Joe Mitchell Chapple

Boss Bart

A Western Story of Love and Politics

Joe Mitchell Chapple

Boss Bart
A Western Story of Love and Politics

ISBN/EAN: 9783744665780

Printed in Europe, USA, Canada, Australia, Japan

Cover: Foto ©Thomas Meinert / pixelio.de

More available books at **www.hansebooks.com**

BOSS BART, POLITICIAN.

A WESTERN STORY OF LOVE AND POLITICS.

BY

JOE MITCHELL CHAPPLE,

Author of "The Minor Chord," Etc.

NEW YORK.
F. Tennyson Neely, Publisher.
1896.

BOSS BART, POLITICIAN.

A Western Story of Love and Politics.

BY

JOE MITCHELL CHAPPLE.

CHAPTER I.

Backward, turn backward,
O, Time, in your flight.
—Old Song, Allen.

It was simply Poplarville, Iowa, according to the United States postoffice directory. One of those rare communities which can scarcely be called a village, and yet pretended to be something more than a mere cross roads. It was a center around which a large number of eastern people and a colony from Indiana had settled in an early day. Quiet, undisturbed by the surging and speculative fever of the quarter century succeeding the civil war, it was just such a spot as to nurture self-reliant childhood and give a tinge of romantic atmosphere to the prosaic career of an Iowa farmer's life. In fact, it represented a distinct type of western farm life.

Two roads started out in a triangle from an old oak tree. This tree, according to the legends of that sec-

tion, was a historical landmark of the Black Hawk
war and was supposed to mark the place where a noted
Indian chieftain fell.   Many cities of the West are said
to have been first located by Indians as camping
grounds, and Poplarville was not an exception to the
rule.   Beside the old oak was its brother, a fallen tree
that had been converted into a rustic seat for loungers
and lovers.   A well and water trough and long hitching post, a small clump of trees on the bank of a creek
in the background, completes the inventory of the
landscape.   The cobbler shop of Jasper Juniper was
located on one side and the cottage of Mary Jane
Toots on the other, and these were the only in-
habited buildings close to this historical spot—but a
number of large farm houses, barricaded by red barns
and granaries, were close at hand.   The very odd angle
of the two roads widening from this historical hub
made it a distinctive point on the map of Iowa, where
rectangles, and only rectangles, marked out farms,
townships and counties, except where a sluggish
stream or lake boundary interfered.   And rectangular
conduct was the reflection of the Puritanic spirit
brought from the East by the early settlers.

These two roads were lined on either side by tall
poplar trees; there were also rail fences, which are one
of the chief landmarks of the industry of the early
pioneers, for rail-splitting has now become a lost art.
The real Iowa road was there—impassable at times,
two deep ruts on either side that suggested a subter-
ranean railroad, always dusty during the dry months.
The road was boulevarded on either side by smart

weeds, milk weeds, pig weeds; in fact, all species of weeds known to botanists and characteristic of deserted and swampy places. The yellow dust from the road settled in clouds upon the weeds and gave some variety of color to the landscape.

But it was not so much the surroundings as the people that distinguished Poplarville from the rest of the world. There seemed to be a grouping of pronounced characters, a mingling of light and shade, without even a suspicion of real villiany on the surface, which made it an interesting community for character study.

It was a sort of composite of all American types.

Poplarville took a special pride in its schools, and the event now most talked of was 'the arrival of the new school teacher, Miss Agnes Agnew, and her advanced ideas on ventilation.

The school board included nearly all of the immediate residents of the corner. There was Judge Tramour, an elegant and refined gentleman of sixty, who had a real and unselfish interest in every pupil; Dr. Buzzer, explosive and vigorous, but kind-hearted; Jasper Juniper, the sage cobbler, who proudly emulated Hans Sachs, of Nurnberg, and was continually reading Plutarch's lives; Abner Tomer, the crusty old bachelor farmer, who held mortgages and his breath for fear of wasting it. The whole community seemed to live together like one large family, with just enough differences, now and then, to suggest a family jar.

The new teacher had ventured to organize a village lyceum, and the selection of one of the girls as presi-

dent came very near causing an open revolt among
the older boys, led by Elbert Ainsworth, a bright and
energetic lad of seventeen.

"We will not submit to petticoat rule," said Elbert
one day after school, and his companions nodded a
mute assent as the teacher was passing just then.
That night the inherent hazing and mob spirit possessed the boys, and tales of the James boys and the
Younger brothers had crept into the village.   Two of
the timid ones who had given some assistance in making feminine rule possible were given a bath under the
old pump at the corners, and were being lustily
bounced in a blanket when Jasper Juniper appeared
and the perpetrators scattered.   The next day there
were mysterious conferences among the pupils,
and Elbert was quite the hero of the hour.   The
event had quelled the spirit of a timid opposition,
and encouraged a mutiny against the pretty and tired
little teacher.

"Elbert Ainsworth will remain after school and be
punished for ungentlemanly conduct," announced the
teacher at the close of that day's session.   There was
a muffled rustle of surprise in the school room, and
Elbert's pride was stung.   He was about to arise and
resent it, but he caught a glimpse of the sparkling
blue eyes of the teacher and saw a spirit of determination.

"I will stay and have some fun with little Miss
Squipps," he whispered to his comrades as they passed
out to the march played on the school organ, another
one of those "new ideas."

But he was mistaken in Agnes Agnew, the teacher.

Not a handsome girl; gentle, flashing blue eyes, a sweet smile and delicate face. A plucky girl of eighteen, determined to make her way in the world. And there was one thing that was intuitively felt by all who met her. She was one whose character or personality seemed to unfold gently at every emergency as acquaintanceship continued. It grew upon one rather than impressed itself by any specific action.

When Elbert and the teacher were left alone, there was an awkward silence.

"Elbert, I must punish you; it was very wrong for you to treat those smaller boys in that way."

"Whip me if you dare," he uttered defiantly. "You will regret it."

"I do regret it now," said the teacher, taking down the whip. "You are too much of a man, too bright a boy to drift into evil ways. Elbert, I love all my pupils, and you will some day be a good man. I had a——" tears started in her eyes, "he was so like you—but now—he is—dead, and I feel so—lonesome."

This seemed to touch his rebellious heart, and Elbert started toward her with a sudden determination.

"Well, teacher, whip me, do your best, do your best. I need it, and I'll never trouble you further."

"I do not want to punish the penitent; it is——"

"You must," broke in Elbert; "now give it to me."

She still hesitated, with the whip in her hand.

"I cannot," she said, breaking into tears and sinking into a chair. "My pupils ought to be ruled by respect instead of by the rod."

"Yes, teacher, but when respect fails, use the rod," said Elbert, coming toward her.

"Never, Elbert; you are a noble boy," she said, rising and dropping the whip. "I felt it, and if you only knew how difficult it is to conduct this school, when the oldest and best pupils are openly rebellious, you would consider my feelings. It is all for your own good."

"I know it, and I'll see that you are not troubled with me any further. Teacher, you are plucky, and you have made me want to be somebody."

"Elbert, you must always obey the instincts of true manhood. Good-night."

As he shook her hand in leaving, he repeated, "Teacher, depend on me hereafter," and she knew he meant it.

When alone in the school room she broke into tears. Her life seemed such a hard struggle, and there is something in the atmosphere and quiet of a school room after a day of trouble and worry that leaves a tinge of sadness in the heart of a teacher.

"Well, it is all for Wesley, and I must keep up."

And then she had another cry for a few minutes, and that seemed to clarify the atmosphere of her troubles.

CHAPTER II.

"'Adieu!' she cried, and waved her lily hand."
Sweet William's Farewell to Black-Eyed Susan.—Gay.

Miss Agnes had only been at the head of the school a short time, and had introduced numerous new ideas. Rules in arithmetic were not to be committed, but stated by pupils in their own language; physics was taught by actual experiments; botany was studied in open fields, with just enough latitude and liberty to give it zest. A library of ten leather-bound volumes of Chambers' Encyclopedia adorned one corner of the school room, formerly deserted to cobwebs. The students were allowed to go to that corner during school hours without asking permission, and they were beginning to distinguish between liberty and license. Each recitation assumed the form of a lecture. There had been some progress in the new order of things, but when Miss Agnes insisted upon ventilating the school room, it occasioned a special meeting of the school board, and the dismissal of the new teacher was narrowly averted.

The unfavorable beginning soon developed into a measure of success. She had won the hearts of nearly all the pupils. The parents and school board were not so easily converted to the breaking away from the old district school conventionalities. But her pupils idolized her so much that remonstrance against Agnes

Agnew and her ideas was futile. The lyceum flourished, and although not officered by the boys, the
Friday night was the eventful night of the week. Elbert Ainsworth then belonged to the class which was
to have the distinction of graduating in June. They
were to receive the first diplomas ever granted by a
Poplarville school—another of Miss Agnew's new de-
partures.

A few months prior to the graduation, Elbert's father died suddenly and left him to comfort the heart-
broken mother. It was a hard blow to him, but it
seemed to be that particular event which made the boy
a man. He now faced the stern realities of life. After
the funeral he was urged by his mother and teacher
to continue his studies and graduate.

"No, I must make my way in the world," he replied
with spirit. "Teacher, this short year of school life
has brought me to a realization of true ambition. You
taught me to think and gave me a real thirst for knowledge."

"Be careful, my boy, you have scarcely begun, and
if you stay here——"

"What! Stay and rust away like other boys, who
are nurtured too close to pleasant homes?" he asked
in a surprised way. "No, I must plunge into the world.
It is hard to leave, but don't worry, mother, you'll
never have to blush for me."

A "farewell party" was given him by his school-
mates, and it was indeed a sad parting—a breaking
of the home ties. The evening's merry-making con-

cluded with "Good-byes" spoken with moistened eyes. The girls all admired Elbert as a hero.

"What will we do with the old cave, Wildy?" asked Sorghum sadly.

"Oh, well, some one else will join you, boys," replied Elbert in a consoling way. But Shandy and Sorghum looked dubious. The cave in the woods which the boys had made a mysterious retreat after the fashion indicated in a species of forbidden literature, was likely to be deserted after the Robin Hood was gone.

One of the last adieus by any of the party was that of the school teacher.

"Now, Elbert, be a man, a pure man. When temptation comes think of your mother and—well—of me. Your old school teacher will always remember kindly her manly boys."

"Yes, Miss Agnew, I may not be great, I may not be rich, but I will be a man," said Elbert.

He walked home with her. It had become a proud distinction among the school boys to be Miss Agnew's escort. As this was Elbert's last night in Poplarville he was accorded the honor. Elbert rather enjoyed the heroic distinction of "leaving home," and talked to the teacher of his great ambitions and hopes.

"Yes, with Abraham Lincoln and the examples of our other great men to give us hope and stimulate us, there is no limit," he continued enthusiastically.

"Don't build your castles without foundations, and be prepared for disappointments; but, Elbert, be true to the noblest ideals of manhood. Good-bye."

"Good-bye, teacher; I will win the spurs yet."

He had been gone but a few minutes when Agnes, who had remained sitting on the porch, took out a photograph, and was looking at it as only a sweetheart can gaze upon the likeness of her absent lover in the serene moonlight, when Paulina Cracovitz, the gypsy washerwoman, appeared bringing the week's washing. Paulina was a good-hearted woman, and although she would leave Poplarville for weeks at a time, nothing was thought of her mysterious ways, and she seemed to prosper in her work.

"Good evening, Paulina; the washing all ready so soon? Now you will want to see a picture of him," she said archly, showing her the picture of Wesley and his adopted brother.

"The fraulein will pardon me—but the gentleman —him standing—the gentleman who wear the hat— you know him, perhaps?" she asked, looking startled as she gazed at the picture.

"Oh, yes, Paulina; he is an old friend of mine."

"Perhaps from the city? A fiancee, it may happen?" asked Paulina, her black eyes snapping.

"You have sharp eyes, Paulina."

"Ah, the fraulein will not wait for me," and Agnes went into the house after bidding Paulina a kind goodnight.

The moon shown down clear on the strange wild face of Paulina as she went up the road.

"And he thinks he escape? Holy Virgin! never, never," she kept mumbling to herself as she hurried along.

It was then quite late, and when near the old tree at the corner she saw "Snakes" sitting on the doorstep of the cottage of Mary Jane Toots. "Snakes" was a half-demented girl of sixteen who had been placed in Mary Jane's keeping by a city orphan's association; she was harmless, a good helper in the housework on the farm, but almost all she could say was "Mother's dead—mother's dead."

She was mumbling in this way when Paulina came up.

"Perhaps the idiot girl; she know a thing—I will break him in des little hand," Paulina said aloud. It startled "Snakes," and she began:

"Mother gave me this; mother's dead; they killed her," she said, taking a small package out of her bosom and looking at it in a vacant way.

"It is pretty, pretty package; give it me," said Paulina.

"No, no, mother's dead; mother gave it me," moaned "Snakes," grasping the package tight to her breast.

"Let me have it?" demanded the gypsy woman, who seemed to hypnotize the demented girl for the moment. There was a short struggle and Paulina obtained the mysterious parcel, and poor "Snakes" could only keep on saying, "Mother's dead, mother's dead." Her nightly wails were so familiar that it did not attract any especial attention nor even awaken Mary Jane.

When Paulina grasped the package it broke open. On the ground the contents lay scattered about; some old letters, a little Bible, and a faded photograph. The two stood staring at each other and at the photograph on the ground for some minutes.

"It is he; Holy Virgin, I will crush him," said the infuriated gypsy, taking up the picture and tying up the bundle for "Snakes."

"Mother's dead, mother's dead," cried the half-witted girl piteously, following the gypsy washerwoman down the lane.

CHAPTER III.

"Ah! Don't you remember the school, Ben Bolt——"
—Thomas Dunn English.

The tranquil life in communities like Poplarville makes it necessary for the people to have something to talk about to keep them from altogether stagnating. And if actual events do not occur with sufficient regularity, busy tongues begin. The episodes between Agnes and Paulina, and later between Paulina and "Snakes," were undoubtedly never related by any one of them; but there seems to be a mysterious way of knowing things in these communities, and the less actually known the more thoroughly it is talked about.

Jasper Juniper put down a pair of boots he had been tapping in his little shop, and looking over his spectacles, he hailed Shandy Gaff in passing.

"Shandy, call the school board." This summons meant three taps on the old bell over Jasper's shop, that did service for fires, funerals and frolics. The neighborhood was naturally all ablaze at once to know the reason for this sudden summons. Mary Jane's shutters across the way came open with a bang, and she at once prepared to go to the old pump for water and incidentally to hear the "doin's of the school board." Jasper took down a volume of Plutarch from the shelf over his head and looked out through the large front door of his shop, swung open to

catch the May breezes, as he had looked upon
Mary Jane for twenty years past. There was a
sort of an expression "it might have been" passed between the two, but the reverie and pantomime was
broken by the arrival of different members of the
school board, who entered Jasper's shop and appro-
priated the various stools and boxes without unneces-
sary ceremony. After the usual confusion, Judge
Tramour, in his calm and dignified way, called the
meeting to order.

"Here, Judge, take this chair," said Jasper, getting up.

" 'Pears as if Jasper must always toady to the judge.
I wouldn't do it," mumbled Abner Tomer from the
corner.

"Well, gentlemen," continued the judge, "this meeting is called at the request of our teacher, who com-
plains of the bad ventilation of the school house."

"Oh, I didn't know it was ventilation she wanted
—I thought it was pure air—so'm told," growled
Abner.

"Humph! don't know the difference," said Shandy
Gaff just outside the door.

"Has any gentleman any suggestion to offer?" inquired the judge.

"Mr. President," said Dr. Buzzer, "I am inclined to
open correspondence with an association of improved
plumbers looking to any offers."

"I say stick to hum," broke in Abner. "If you
want more air, open the windows. She keeps them
shut, so'm told."

"Abner, you are always behind the times," said Jasper. "Now, Bacon says the gray matter in the brain——"

"I don't care whether bacon, liver or lights says it," broke in Abner.

"Gentlemen, you are wandering away from the subject," interposed the judge.

"Well, I move that our secretary be empowered to consult leading authorities on ventilation. They know the latest improved methods—always said so," said Dr. Buzzer, feeling that he had fully settled the matter.

Just then Mary Jane came out of her cottage and stood listening to the discussion.

"I say old ways suit me," said Mary Jane with emphasis. "Open the windows and doors, march the children around three times—shut the windows, and there you are."

"Judge, I say give the teacher her own way; get what she wants; you see, each scholar ought to have the privilege to breathe his own air and no one else's," piped Shandy through the door.

"Shandy, sit down; you are not a member of this board," said Dr. Buzzer, taking him by the shoulder.

'Got more sense than some of 'em," commented Mary Jane, starting for another pail of water.

"I'd like to go to school, but mother's dead, mother's dead," said "Snakes," as she sat on the doorstep shelling peas.

It was here that Farmer Chatsworth first spoke. He was a new-comer, and by reason of having rented

Housle's farm, and of buying Jordan's four forties just
south, he was given a place on the school board; but
his chief distinction was, however, in being the father
of two handsome daughters, Allie and Veo. He had
removed from a point only eight miles distant, and
yet he was looked upon as something of a stranger.

"Well, gentlemen, I believe in improvements; I
vote as the doctor votes—I must go, as my folks are
coming, you know," said Chatsworth cheerily.

"So'm told," punctured Abner with a sneer.

"Jasper just read them the law from Plutarch; see
how the ancient Romans managed ventilation; human lungs are the same to-day as then," said the jolly
farmer as he left."

"Always said so," chimed in Buzzer.

"Roman cranks and Iowa cranks line up pretty
much alike," gurgled Shandy outside.

"Has any gentleman any resolution to offer?" inquired the judge.

"I move that ventilation be laid under the table,"
snarled Abner.

"Is there a second?" inquired the judge, waiting.

There was nothing but silence.

"Before you go any further," said Jasper, "I've a
letter which I think will settle the business for the
present—when Plutarch——"

"Please read the letter, Jasper," interposed the
judge.

"To the Honorable Board of Education"—ahem
—"I hereby resign my position as teacher of the Pop-

larville school, the resignation to take effect immediately. Signed, Agnes Agnew."

The announcement came like a thunderbolt upon the meeting.

"Going to be married, by gosh," said Shandy, jumping up.

"Another fool going to yoke up," said Mary Jane, dropping a pail of water.

"And mother's dead," broke in "Snakes."

"Should lose her sometime—always said so," said the doctor, emphatically.

"I move the resignation be accepted," said Jasper.

"The contract runs for another year, so'm told," objected Abner.

Just then Miss Agnes was seen coming down the road, and the judge hailed her.

"I say, Miss Agnes, can't you wait another year and complete your contract?" said the judge, with a gallant and courteous bow.

"Judge, there is a personal reason why I cannot do so. I love my work, but—there is a reason—Judge—and I'm sure——" said Agnes, hesitatingly and half blushing. But it did not take long for each individual member of the board to surmise the secret.

"Gentlemen, if there are no objections, Miss Agnew's resignation is accepted," said the judge.

"You have made the school a great success, always said so," echoed Dr. Buzzer, "and we hope your pathway will be strewn with good deeds, lovely flowers, and all the peace and happiness any—well, any life can bring," continued the doctor, with a profound and courtly bow, imitating the gallantry of the judge.

The school board meeting adjourned sine die, the stately judge escorting the pretty school teacher up the lane to the Chatsworth farm house, where she was stopping.

Now Poplarville did have something to talk about.

CHAPTER IV.

"What man dares, I dare."

—Macbeth.

It was a favorite pastime for the judge, Jasper and Dr. Buzzer to talk over old days and new problems in the old cobbler shop. "We transplant the bone and sinew of the city from the country," was the verdict agreed upon. Abner was not there often, as he did not quite fall in with the open and candid method of discussion, and somehow the finding of that mysterious photograph by the gypsy washerwoman had come to his ears, and it seemed to give him a secret satisfaction, as he went about with the expression of a Modred.

Elbert's departure for Chicago had been the theme of discussion in the cobbler shop, and grave doubts were expressed by the Poplarville triumvirate as to whether a scrupulously honest boy like Elbert could gain a foothold in Chicago.

"There's such a thing as being too extremely honest," said the doctor at the close of one of the discussions.

"Yes, but the heads of most of the great mercantile institutions of the city and many of its leading professional men were born in the country. They have lived close to the soil, and have that spirit of self-reliance of which city children are deprived. Nearly every country boy who goes to the city to make a place

for himself knows this intuitively, and comes well
armed with a fixed purpose. He concentrates, origin-
ates and succeeds—sometimes," said the judge, watching Jasper giving a final tap to a shoe before throwing
it down.

It was early in March when Elbert arrived in Chicago. The cold, bleak winds swept from the lake, chill-
ing to the marrow. The pavements, checkered with
dark pools of ice, and the black mud gave anything but
a pleasant tinge to Elbert's first impressions of the
streets of Chicago. The trees in the parks seemed so
scattered and bare. The rush and rattle of traffic, the
apparently heartless struggle on the crowded streets,
and the dull weather made him feel the first real pangs
of homesickness. He studied the newspapers for a
situation and made numerous applications to the addresses indicated for employment as waiter, porter,
hostler, elevator boy, etc., but each time he was turned
away with the remark that they wanted experienced
city help.

"Am I not fit for something?" he thought as he
passed up Dearborn street in the evening at six o'clock,
when all the clerks were hurrying homeward.   Into
many of the strange faces he looked as if expecting to
see some one from Poplarville. There were some who
looked like Jasper, the judge, or the doctor.   There
was one that looked like Shandy—but it was not he.
He wondered if they all had happy homes—and mothers.   y

Hunting for a cheap boarding house, he stopped at a
nest of vice, but his mother's and teacher's words rang

in his ears, and he would scarcely look into a saloon as he rushed by. The next morning and the next he continued his search for work, but had no success. A week later he was employed in carrying bricks on an office building being erected. It was hard work, but he was busy and earning money. He was just taking the pressed bricks out of a cart when he heard some one hail him.

"Hello, El, bricks without straw; well, I never!"

It was Ned Housle, the brother of Kittie Housle, Elbert's childhood sweetheart. His pride was stung at first, but he replied, "Yes, it is better than buying gold bricks."

Ned was one of those fast young men who had often come to Chicago using his father's money to see the sights, and he was regarded as quite a hero in Poplarville, but only a short time ago he had lost a large amount of money through card sharks."

"Well, you won't be so funny after awhile, young man," continued Ned. "Come around to-night and we'll take in the sights by gas-light."

"Thank you, Ned, but I'll have to sleep to hold this situation."

"All right; you're a trifle green, but you'll have the rough corners smoothed off later."

Ned passed on. Elbert was so glad to see any one from home that he carried bricks with a lighter heart, even if it was only Ned Housle whom he had seen; but that Kittie's brother should find him a hod carrier naturally stung his boyish pride.

That afternoon he dropped a hod of bricks; the contractor happened to be inspecting the work just then.

"Discharge that greenhorn, Jim," he said to the foreman. "He'll be dropping bricks on some one's head yet and bring us a damage suit."

Contractor Bart Waldie was a little, short man, with curly hair and stubby mustache. His black eyes snapped, and it was evident that he was a thorough organizer. He not only employed superintendents, but superintended superintendents and watched every detail of the work.

Elbert was discharged as an incompetent hod carrier. Three months of hunting for work, with only an occasional day of employment, nearly absorbed his earnings, and he conceived the idea of saving what little he had left for meals by sleeping in a railway station,where he had noticed that immigrants remained for the night on their way west. He had cuddled up on a hard seat in a dark corner, slipping himself under the iron arms, and was soon sweetly dreaming of his mother and home. Later on a policeman shook him.

"Where are you going, young man?"

"To sleep, if I can," said Elbert, drowsily.

"Well, I think not, sir; come, get up; you'll have to move out of this."

"But I've no place else to sleep."

"That's the old fake. Well, then, come to the station."

"The police station?" said Elbert, now thoroughly astonished and awakened. "I've done nothing, and you can't take me."

"I can't; well, I'll show you, honey. Come along, and no talk back."

"I won't do it."

"Yes, you will."

At that he motioned as if to strike Elbert with his club. Elbert struck back and they clinched. Another policeman arrived and they soon had Elbert on the way to the station. As they passed the great massive buildings, Elbert wondered if these were really the habitations of human beings. Was there no place for a wanderer except in jail? These were Elbert's bitter thoughts as he was hurried along.

In jail! What would his mother think! What would his teacher think! And how could he explain it? As he mingled with the motley crowd of vagabonds Elbert felt that the world was entirely wrong. His reflections were such as lead to anarchy as the only possible solution. Whose wealth is all this? Who has the right to invoke law and punish the homeless for the crime of poverty? After a quiet cry his bitterness subsided. He was now facing the stern realities of life. How happy those boys at home after all, even if they were only drifting along in an aimless and useless existence, lounging on dry goods boxes and along sunny sides of street corners.

The next morning was a bright and beautiful day in early June. He recalled the fact that this was the day he would have graduated from the village school with flowers and a diploma. The odor of the station was stifling, and he felt a relief as he was brought into the court room before the justice.

"My boy," said the judge, "you are charged with resisting an officer. Are you guilty?"

"I resisted him because he struck me."

"Go on with you, that's a——" broke in Officer Flaherty.

"Silence! I'm hearing this case," interjected the court.

"Were you drunk or disorderly?" he continued.

"No, sir; I was only trying to sleep, and—and— what will mother think?" he said, with moistened eyes.

"The old gag again," chimed in the policeman.

"Will you be quiet, Flaherty," sternly demanded the judge. "What did you find on the prisoner's person?"

"Sixty cents, sir, and this little book."

"My mother's Bible," broke in Elbert, excitedly.

"The old Bible fake again," mumbled Flaherty.

The judge looked at the Bible, read the inscription on the fly leaf, and said: "Discharge the prisoner and erase his name from the docket."

CHAPTER V.

"Mastering the lawless science of our law,
That codeless myriad of precedent,
That wilderness of single instances."
—Tennyson.

Leaving the court room, Elbert breathed a sigh of relief, and yet he was filled with bitter thoughts, and was almost tempted to give up the struggle to gain a foothold in Chicago and return home. At the post-office he found a letter from his mother. It was filled with delightful little incidents of home life. "There is no one here to help me with my work as you used to do, but everything goes on all right, although I miss you so much. By the way," concluded the letter, "Miss Agnew is about to be married, and will live at —— Wabash Avenue, and she said you must call and see them. She has inquired often about you, and said that the graduation class did not seem complete without Elbert. I enclose one of the programmes. Kittie Housle looked very sweet in her new graduation dress and quite carried off the honors. There is lots more news I would like to tell you, but be a good boy and write often to mother."

He felt there was a rift in the clouds in anticipating the arrival of his teacher in Chicago, but here again pride interposed. His clothes were not such as to indicate that he was getting on very well. He made another attempt to secure employment, and through the kindly interest of a teacher in a mission Sunday school he was given the position of assistant janitor in a public library. His patron was delighted to find him a few days later apparently absorbed in a volume of Shakespeare. The truth must be confessed that Elbert managed to have the volume conspicuously in sight as his patron approached.

"Good reading makes good men," said his patron, approvingly.

The position was the turning point in Elbert's Chicago career. The story of Lincoln studying by the light of pine knots inspired him, and every spare moment was concentrated upon the best reading. Once his real thirst for knowledge was known he found plenty of helpers, and his identification with Sunday school and church work soon made him feel quite at home.

*   *   *   *   *   *   *   *   *

He became so absorbed in his ambition that he was careless about writing home, and had almost ceased thinking of his old school teacher and her expected arrival in Chicago. Nearly a year had elapsed since the morning his mother had first written him of the marriage, and she now recalled the fact by giving her name as Mrs. Bartlett Waldie, Wabash Avenue, and saying that the wedding had occurred only a short time before, instead of a year previous, as he had supposed.

He found the house one of those convenient and comfortable homes in Chicago in a district or locality almost as isolated as in a village. The routine of life consisted of a visit to the grocery, meat market, and bakery each day, an occasional call for cough drops at the pharmacy, a trip now and then down town; the monotony of life almost as fixed as that of the country.

Elbert was met at the door, as he walked up the polished front steps, by the contractor who had discharged him as an incompetent hod carrier; but fortunately, as he thought, Mr. Waldie apparently did not recognize him.

"Well, Elbert, how are those spurs?" said Mrs. Waldie, after she introduced her husband. Elbert was enthusiastic and buoyant in his hopes, and told of what he had been studying and reading.

"It's all due to your teaching," he said to Mrs. Waldie, with his city acquired bow.

They spent a delightful evening. Bart Waldie was quite taken with Elbert as a bright and energetic young fellow, and from that on he had a standing invitation to spend his Sundays at the Waldies, and the influence of that home life was of great moment and value in determining his career.

"Young man, you ought to study law," said Waldie in the course of his conversation some time later.

"But how can I? It takes money. No matter how much brains and ambition a young man may have, he cannot put that up as collateral at Chicago banks."

"But there are always those ready to help deserving young men."

"Yes, but poor relations come first, and it is only by chance that deserving young men are known."

"Well, I am going to help you," said Bart, reflectively.

"How can I ever thank you—"

"Don't try it until you know what I am going to do."

"If it is only a chance I shall never forget it."

"Well, Mrs. Waldie has thought perhaps if you had an opportunity to study law you would succeed. You have a good imagination, I should judge, from the fairy stories you have been telling us. Oh, yes, I know boys. Well, Ainsworth, I have faith in you."

"You are very kind, sir, and I shall hope to merit your confidence."

"Never fear, my gospel is simple—always stick to your friends."

"Trust me for that, Mr. Waldie," said Elbert, as they shook hands warmly and parted.

Waldie had just begun a political career in a small way, and had met with some success. He liked Elbert, and saw in him just such a young man as he needed. At the last election Waldie had been placed in charge of a ward and had carried it for his party. He went at it systematically and scientifically, and the fascination of politics had crept upon him, as he had just succeeded through political influence in defeating a rival firm in bidding on a large contract. In fact, he was becoming one of the powers at the City Hall. He was a clever fellow, and every voter in his division was known to him, and, being a contractor and practical workman, "Bart" was a favorite with the workingmen, and was proudly pointed to as a man who "stays by his friends." Of course many of his allies were saloon men, but Bart had held aloof from them to some extent in personal affairs.

"I need a young fire-alarm talker, and Ainsworth is going to fill the bill," thought Waldie, and he prided himself on his judgment of men.

He was talking over his determination with his wife.

"You are very kind, Bart, and he is a noble boy."

"I knew it would please you, my dear, and we must help him. I like young fellows with that kind of stuff in them."

That night Elbert was too happy to sleep. Visions of Daniel Webster and Sumner came before him, and he arose at midnight and wrote a long letter to his mother.

"Waldie's politics," he told her, "are different from father's, but perhaps parties are only a matter of taste after all, because I am determined to enlist under the banner of my new found friend."

Elbert began his law studies in earnest. With Blackstone and Kent's Commentaries, occasional night lectures and training under an old practitioner, he made good progress. It was, however, a hard struggle. The irksome drudgery made it necessary for him to literally tie himself to his chair and remain at his tasks. His student days were not marked by any events of a striking nature, no theaters nor luxuries, and not even a visit home.

"Mother, I am coming home when I can hang up my shingle as a lawyer," he wrote in each of his letters. And when he walked out of the court room a full-fledged lawyer, pinching himself vigorously to try to realize what it was to be a real lawyer, he was quite surprised to find that he felt no different than usual.

He looked up to Bart as a father, and no longer felt the pangs of being a stranger in the city. Yes, life seemed to open with bright prospects for him, and like all ambitious young men, he thought more, perhaps, of a sweet little face at the old home than he would like to have confessed.

CHAPTER VI.

"Thou should'st not judge fully of a man's life before he
dieth, whether it should be called blessed or wretched."
—Sophocles.

To a picturesque Indiana village Chalmers Agnew
came with his bride from Kentucky to make a home
and to start in life.   It was a time when there was bitter strife in Hoosierdom between the new and the old
order of things.   The young bride came with silk
dresses, veils and gloves, which quite shocked the community in their intense religious beliefs, and their actions made it so decidedly uncomfortable for the young
wife that she soon gave up her finery and became "like
one of us, children of the Lord."   The first Sunday at
the little chapel at Mount Ariel struck terror to the
heart of the newcomer.   The hymn,

> "I've enlisted for the war,
> And will fight until I die,"

was sung in an intensely realistic manner, and one
exhorting missionary induced the young wife to put
her handsome earrings in the contribution box, to be
sold to help the heathen.

As time went on they adapted themselves to the new
order of things, but the husband drifted into reading
Tom Paine's books, and it was secretly whispered
about the village that he possessed a set of Voltaire's

works. He was said to have joined an infidel society at Indianapolis, where he had served in the State Legislature.

One day when Agnes, their only child, was about five years old, Chalmers Agnew was injured while chopping down a tree. "A visitation of the Lord" was the general verdict among the church people. As he lay dying, mysterious nurses came from Indianapolis; the neighbors were alarmed and superstitious about caring for an infidel, as if there were the danger of an infectious disease. The nurses kept away outsiders, and it was said to be for the purpose of preventing Agnew from "confessing the Lord on his deathbed." Just before he died, an appealing glance to his wife and daughter told them the story. It was a good-bye to meet again. He was denied a funeral service, also a grave in the little burying ground in the rear of the chapel; and on the following Sunday the preacher thundered out in his sermon a bitter denunciation of "that pernicious infidel, Agnew." This was the consolation offered the sorrowing widow. Mrs. Agnew did not long survive her husband. With Wesley Walker, another orphan, little Agnes was adopted into the family of a generous farmer named Waldie, and the two children were as his own. His own son, Bart, and Wesley were inseparable companions, and Agnes their playmate. They were all educated as well as the means of the farmer would permit. When the boys were about twenty years of age they left for Chicago to make their fortunes, having learned the building trade. Wesley and Agnes were to be married when

Wesley had secured a competence. At first the two plucky boys prospered, and then reverses came and delayed the marriage, and Wesley wrote: "I want a home for my wife when we are married. Never mind, Agnes, it will soon come out all right."

It was after this reversal of fortune that Agnes had concluded to assist by teaching the village school at Poplarville, Iowa. When she had finished the first year of school in that village, Wesley brought her to the house of a friend in Chicago. They were to be married in their own home on the following day, and immediately on their arrival had gone to inspect the new house.

"I am so happy, Agnes," said Wesley, as they entered the new cottage. "Every time Bart and I came here to inspect the work we thought of you."

The young girl was supremely happy. It seemed so like a bright beginning of life after all.

"Mother is coming, too," broke in Bart. Won't it be a jolly family, Aggie? Wes. is so excited that he had almost forgotten mother."

"No, I never could forget her. Now, Bart, you'll have a place to spend your bachelor days in peace and comfort."

Bart left, and Wesley stooped and kissed the blushing girl. "My own noble Agnes! I am so happy!" Arm in arm they walked about inspecting the rooms, filled with the fragrant odor of new lumber.

"Here's where you can put your china, and drawers for the linen—no water to carry. Isn't it snug, Agnes?"

"Wesley, you are so kind and thoughtful. This large window for the birds, here the piano, and there the picture of mamma." With a woman's instinct she had it all planned at a glance.

"Wesley, I can scarcely realize it all. Is this our home?"

"Yes, dear," he said proudly, "our home, "and we'll be so happy, won't we?"

"The flowers!" exclaimed Agnes, as she saw beautiful roses nodding in the large window of the basement dining room, protected by iron bars.

"How sweet is life, Wesley! A home—our home!" continued Agnes, radiant in her happiness.

CHAPTER VII.

"Or ope the sacred source of sympathetic tears."
—The Progress of Poesy, Thos. Gray.

If there is one thing the average American newspaper reader loves to feast upon, it is a mysterious murder case. Chicago has furnished its full quota. The people were startled the following day by reading of the murder of Wesley Walker, the young contractor. He was found in his office that morning dead, having evidently been killed by a blow on the head with a stone bottle containing writing fluid. The safe had been robbed and it was apparently the work of burglars whom he had discovered. Bart had waited for him that night at their room later than usual, but he supposed Wesley had remained with Agnes talking over the arrangements for the wedding on the morrow. He was shocked to find his brother and partner in the morning stretched dead on the floor of the office, and immediately offered a large reward for the arrest of the murderer. Black footprints from the spilled ink and blood were traced some distance and then lost. The mystery was difficult to solve. Several arrests were made on a chain of strong circumstantial evidence, but the murderers had covered their tracks well. Agnes was prostrated by the terrible tragedy; the mother, Mrs. Waldie, only arrived in time that morning to return with the funeral cortege instead of join-

ing a happy bridal party as she had anticipated.
Wesley's remains were taken back to the old home at
Mount Ariel, Indiana. Agnes and her adopted mother were accompanied by Bart, who proved a noble and
generous companion in their distress and did all in his
power to comfort them. He remained a few days at
the old home.

"Wesley, Wesley," cried Agnes as she looked about
and saw many things to remind her of her lover.

"It was a hard blow, little sis," said Bart, "but we
must always be prepared for trials."

Bart returned to Chicago and prospered, making
frequent visits home. Agnes and his mother looked
forward with great pleasure to Bart's visit, as he was
always so kind and thoughtful. The sudden blow which
bereft him of a brother upon whom he had so much
depended in his struggle for success had left its impress and his frequent visits and letters did much to
allay the bitter grief of Agnes; in fact the death of
Wesley brought them all closer together.

One evening at twilight nearly a year after Wesley's
death Bart and Agnes walked down the old lane at Mt.
Ariel where with Wesley they had spent so many happy days in childhood.

"How pleasant it is to be at the old home again,"
said Bart. "Let's sit down, Aggie. I want to talk to
you. Now, Aggie, that property in Chicago is yours
just as much as though poor Wesley were alive.
His interest in the business remains the same—the
same as if you had been married."

"Oh, Bart, you are too generous," said Agnes, looking up through her tears. "It was so sudden, his death prostrated me—cruelly murdered. Who could have been so wicked, so heartless? Poor Wesley, love's young dream has faded away—one single night between the fullest happiness and the saddest woe—O, Wesley, Wesley."

"It was a hard blow for me, Aggie, his bright young face, his enthusiasm, made him the leader in our business. He never failed to make friends and our profits were large," said Bart in a consoling way.

"Why should God make my life so miserable? Sometimes I feel bitter against the world—"

"There are others, Aggie."

"Yes, yes, we mourn together our brother—our playmate, you have been a noble friend to him."

"Agnes, Agnes—I—I—" said Bart passionately, drawing close to her.

"Why, Bart, what is it, you look pale—come let us go on."

"Agnes, let me take Wesley's place, but truly I love you; let me—"

"Bart, I must be honest; my heart, my life was given to Wesley; his death leaves it blank."

"Agnes, I do not ask you to forget our brother, but in the struggle of life I am so lonely—so lonely," he said, breaking into tears.

"Bart, a woman is never dead to sympathy, and your tears are more eloquent than—"

"They come from the heart," broke in Bart, earnestly, and as we were children together let us be man and woman together."

"You are so good and true, Bart; it is hard for a
woman to transfer suddenly real love, but perhaps in
time—"

"Say yes, Agnes," he pleaded.

"But I have accepted my old place as teacher at
Poplarville."

"Leave that to take care of itself; there you are carrying on an unequal struggle all alone; you are trying to
introduce new ideas—some common sense among
those dumb people; leave it all and come home; write
your resignation now."

"But Bart, the school board will never forgive me;
there is a year's contract."

"With me, Agnes, it is a life contract. One word
from you now decides my destiny."

"Bart, it seems too bad to break—"

"Say yes, Agnes," and he suddenly kissed her, not
as he had often done before, but in the solemn twilight
that kiss was a lover's token. Half consenting, she
consented; a few weeks later they were married at
the old home and left soon after for Chicago.

CHAPTER VIII.

"A politician; one that would circumvent God."
—Hamlet.

Shortly after Bart and Agnes were settled in Chicago, Elbert had called upon them and found his new friend, whose gospel, "stand by your friends," made a lasting impression upon him. Bart Waldie's business flourished as his political success advanced; in fact the flush of commercial prestige resulted in a deeper fascination for politics until now it had become almost a part of his business.

"Bart, I don't like politics," said his wife one day shortly after, "there are so many temptations."

"Trust me Agnes," he said laughing. "Elbert and I are going to reform political methods in Chicago. He is a bright young fellow and a natural politician."

"Yes, but I am afraid of the pitfalls."

"Tut, tut, that's the old notion. Why in a few years you women will be voting, and then I'm going to run for office."

"Bart, when our influence at home is extinguished we shall ask for the ballot, not till then."

"Sensible wife. Now I must hurry to catch the train for Springfield. We have an important bill there to look after. Elbert is going with me."

"Bart, take care of the boy; don't let him—"

"Come Agnes, don't you worry over Elbert. He

has a long, wise head, and a wise, long-headed young
man never gets himself into trouble. Good-bye,
dear."

Elbert accompanied Bart to Springfield, and was
introduced by him into the arena of practical state
politics. There was a special bill then pending before
the legislature to amend the city charter so as to enable
the manipulation of certain valuable franchise rights
and privileges. The champagne suppers came thick
and fast. The bill was lobbied under the pretense of
being in the interest of the city and the lobby expenses in part were liquidated by the city under various
guises. Money was spent with the freedom characteristic of American commercial operations. It was the
modern mania for boodling that asserted itself. Yankee "shrewdness" demanded a victim, and if none other
were possible the public treasury must suffer even
though as a tax-payer the irrepressible Yankee spirit
was in fact robbing itself. Axes were there to be
ground with silver and gold, and influence was largely
measured by moneyed interests. Men who stood on
street corners crying most vehemently for reform had
their franchise irons well into the fire.

A glimpse behind the scenes made Elbert shudder
as he noted the actions of mysterious groups in hotel
corridors.

"Bart, is this practical politics? Is all this legislation pernicious?"

"Disgusting, isn't it, my boy? Well, some consider
it so, but it is not half so bad as it looks. The money
is used to get bad men to refrain from defeating good

measures as well as to get good men to vote for bad measures."

"Well, monarchy is not so bad after all. One boodling prince is better than a pack of princely boodlers."

"Oh, well, you'll get over those exaggerated notions, my boy. Come with me to 48."

They went upstairs to room 48 and there found two clerks of a railway company busy making out passes. The room was filled with state law-makers. On the mantel was a bottle of whisky and other transparent indications of hospitality. In an inner room sat the kingly lobbyist with his arms gently about one of the "boys," talking over the bill which was to come before the legislature on the following day.

"O, yes, he is our friend," said the lobbyist, coming out with his hands on the shoulders of two members and talking very earnestly.

"Well, Bart, old boy, how are you?" was his greeting, and Elbert was introduced to the inner circle of our great sovereign government, of, for, and by the people.

Shades of Lincoln, all this at the threshold of his sacred tomb!

They had returned home and Elbert was impressed with new ideas of our great government, and he said little as he and Bart sat alone together. Elbert was planning for an evening of music when there was a ring at the door and a card sent in.

"Mrs. Daniels of Washington," said Bart. "O, yes, Senator Forthwith—"

Elbert took the hint and left before the lady was shown in.

"Mrs. Daniels of Washington; pray be seated," said Bart, gallantly, as he greeted a handsome woman strikingly dressed. She swept into the room with an air of superb ease and confidence.

"I have called, Mr. Waldie, at the request of Senator Forthwith of the Appropriations Committee, with this letter of introduction. You will notice that the Senator desires your co-operation in a little matter affecting the River and Harbor bill," she said in an easy and business-like way.

"Yes."

"I learned confidentially before leaving Washington that your chances for the marshalship are remarkably good; you will likely be appointed, and I am instructed to ask you to carry out the provisions of that letter."

"Thank you; let me see," said Bart, consulting the letter. "Check two thousand dollars, personal expenses of Mrs. Daniels, um! Letter from me recommending Mrs. Daniels to the governor of Wisconsin, um! Two thousand dollars; is that the lowest, Mrs. Daniels?"

"It should be twice as much."

"Um, and what do I get in return, do you say?"

"Well, there will be ten men on the pay roll of public works, two consulships, small of course, one clerkship in the Interior Department, and our influence."

Agnes entered the room just then. Bart went toward her.

"Ah, my wife; Mrs. Daniels of Washington, my dear."

"From Washington? A beautiful city. Do you make a long stay in Chicago?" said Agnes.

"No, I am here only a few days; that is, here and Springfield. By the way, Mr. Waldie, I met in Springfield a charming young man—Mr. Ainsworth—he mentioned your name.

"Oh, yes, a bright young fellow, one of my wife's former pupils," said Bart with an air of pride.

"Ah," continued Mrs. Daniels, "I took quite a fancy to him, but his ideas politically are too visionary for success: silk-stocking methods. Well, you know, sentiment is all very well, but the pocket-book is the only sentiment the voter and worker understand."

"Why, Mrs. Daniels, I am surprised," broke in Agnes; "I thought Mr. Ainsworth's views the most sensible for pure government and entirely shared by my husband."

Bart moved uneasily in his chair, and Mrs. Daniels gave a quick look from one to the other and entirely comprehended the situation.

"Ah, my dear Mrs. Waldie, I fear pure government is chimerical," said the charming widow with a wave of her gloved hand.

"Politics, my dear, must be practical," said Bart.

"And if the women voted—" said Agnes.

"Then they would not be practical. I will call at five, Mr. Waldie, for your answer," said Mrs. Daniels, arising to go.

"We shall be pleased to see you, and you will be just

in time then for a cup of tea," said Agnes, going with her to the door.

As Agnes returned, her question to Bart was quite the natural interrogation of a curious wife. "Who is this Mrs. Daniels, Bart?"

"A friend of Senator Forthwith."

"Ah, a lobbyist, of course. Bart, give up politics and attend to business. It will sooner or later make great changes in you and me; it is an unnatural life; the product of false position, and the golden opportunity under our present methods of government of rascals and thieves. Give it up."

The mail was brought in just then and Bart busied himself looking it over hurriedly, and continued:

"There pet, don't worry. I love you enough to do almost anything you ask. I expect to-day to be appointed U. S. Marshal. Yes, by George, here is the envelope; we will soon be in clover. Perhaps I shall be elected governor; who knows. Then you will be Mrs. Governor Waldie, eh?"

But the political prospects did not seem to inspire Agnes; there was a pained and sad look on her face as Elbert entered to help Bart with the mail.

"Here is a letter from Thompson from the North Side; wants you to attend to Simpkins' bill for carriages; it has been hanging over since the primaries," said Elbert, busy at his work.

"Any letter for me, Bart?" said Agnes.

"No, no, dear, don't bother me just now, I am busy" said Bart, with an air of impatience. "McCutcheon says," continued Bart to Elbert, "we want to

show ourselves at the opening of the A. B. C. on
Madison street; take in Hooley's great show and
wind up on the roof garden; then he has arranged for
us to quiet Madigan; you know Madigan? Little Jim-
mie of North Clark street, at 10 o'clock and at 1
o'clock; we are to meet at Madame Porteo's roof garden of course; she has the pull in the Second Precinct
of her ward.

"Bart, I am tired and sick of this all-night, meet-me-
in-the-dark work. It is disreputable. Is there no
such thing as clean politics?" said Elbert, with impatience.

Bart, wheeling around in his chair answered very
shortly:

"Noap, noap, Elbert, you are my right-hand man;
you know who made you; stick by your friends."

"Well, I am sticking to you."

"Our fences got down a little when I went to Springfield; we must prop them up."

"All right," said Elbert, resignedly, "but as I said in
Springfield the other day, I would give two years of
my life to find twenty honest men in a bunch in any
political gathering."

"Political success means political enemies; you accepted a retainer in that corporation affair. Well the
labor vote is against you now."

"It was simply a fair and honest retainer in my profession."

"Um! and they call you a boodler because you took
that city fee."

"Well, I earned it and you got it for me."

"That doesn't matter.   O, well, I just wanted you to become hardened to these things.   You see honest dealings are sometimes more difficult to explain than open stealing.   Now I see McCutcheon and Schledgmilch are here; you better go while I straighten out matters on the German vote."

CHAPTER IX.

"This divorcive law."
　　　　　　　　　　　　—Milton.

After having been admitted to the bar, Elbert had plunged into the real struggle of building up a law practice. As fate decreed it, he had an office in the very building for which he had carried brick. It was one of those large office buildings which contained more people than all the inhabitants of the village of Poplarville. Bart sent him considerable business to start with through political friends. His library at first consisted of black-bound government reports, blue books, and the other tonnage of dead literature so generously distributed by the government. As volume by volume was added to his law library, he gained an acquaintanceship with them more or less thorough. His speeches at political conventions and caucuses throughout the city attracted general attention, and he soon became an invaluable and loyal lieutenant to Bart. He joined secret societies enthusiastically, and became a popular, companionable fellow; but his social and political success naturally caused a coterie of bitter enemies.

Soon after he visited his mother at the old home in Poplarville. How proud he felt as the old friends of childhood now referred to him as a Chicago lawyer;

and he felt that his Charles Summer side-whiskers
gave him a particularly distinguished appearance.

"I always knew that boy would make his mark, by
ginger," said Dr. Buzzer. "These other youngsters
staid at home tied to their mother's apron strings.
Now just see the difference."

During this visit home Elbert secured his first case.
Ned Housle, the brother of his old sweetheart, had
married Nettie Jackson, the only daughter of a
wealthy farmer living near the village. Young
Housle's taste for city life had led him to Chicago,
where he had squandered nearly all of his wife's money in trying to establish himself on the Chicago Board
of Trade. His natural instincts were those of the
gambler, and now that his money was gone the faithful wife had gone to Chicago to try and help him. Her
reward was a suit for divorce, Housle thinking that to
avoid publicity and trouble the deserted wife would
allow the case to go by default.

Not so the irate father, who was a friend of Dr.
Buzzer.

"I'd never stand it, by ginger! That young scape-
grace should be taught a lesson. I'd fight it," declared the doctor.

"Yes, but where's the money to hire one of those
expensive city lawyers," said his friend plaintively.

"Why, hire young Ainsworth. He's a fighter with
good spurs. He's got to win his epaulets, and he'll
fix him, always said so."

Elbert was seen and promptly took the case, feeling in it a chivalrous duty as well as an opportunity.

He went at it systematically to study the evidence.
Notes were made of all important points and jotted
down in the peculiar way of a lawyer. A leaf tran-
scribed from his note book appeared as follows:
"Cruelty
April 2—back door—hit club
Child—Buzzer—Phys.—Career—
Chicago—gamb.—mist—Scrog.—
Shandy—good char."
and so on page after page.

The declaration had been served and Elbert had only
a few days in which to file his answer, which was a general denial, with a counter-charge of inhuman treat-
ment. He threw his whole soul into the effort, working night and day, and did not forget the important
feature—the jury. In this Bart's general acquaintance
and influence was favorable. While there was no direct statement made of the fact, it was generally understood that young Ainsworth should have "the right
jury."

The day of the trial arrived and the court room was
filled with a large throng expecting an array of deli-
cious scandal. The sensational newspapers reported
it fully, and Bart saw to it that the artists and reporters
gave due prominence to the "bright young attorney for
the defense."

The preliminary proceedings were completed, and
although older lawyers opposed him and Bart had offered to secure help, Elbert insisted on fighting the
case alone. He struck from the panel of the jury
such men as were thought to be unfavorable, under

Bart's whispered directions. The wife and her father sat near him, and the husband, flashily attired, was defiant and unconcerned across the table. The features of the trial were the frequent objections and exceptions by Elbert, his copious notes, and a few stern reprimands from the court. His cross-examination was so different from the usual stereotyped method that it rather nonplussed his opponents, and his witnesses gave such simple and brief testimony that it left Housle's attorneys but little to work upon. The evidence had all been taken and it seemed a clear case for the defense, as general sympathy was naturally with the wife. The village neighbors from Iowa had proven her character beyond reproach and also the brutality of the husband. To Elbert everything seemed serene for a verdict, and he was busy gathering notes for an eloquent final plea.

"We will call Peter Scroggins for further cross-examination," said one of Housle's attorneys.

This was a surprise to Elbert, as Scroggins had been one of his strongest witnesses.

"You swore, Mr. Scroggins, that you saw Housle strike the defendant at the rear door of their home on the morning of the 2d of April last?"

"Yes, sir; I did."

"Now, sir; tell us what was the provocation of that blow."

"I object," shouted Elbert.

"She had run away with Bill Bozeman," Scroggins answered quickly.

"I move that be stricken out," continued Elbert.

There was a ripple of excitement in the court room over this sensational evidence. The judge was trying to quiet the crowd, while Peter, turning to the jury, continued:

"Bill Bozeman is dead now, but he was a tough one."

The little wife broke into tears and the father turned white and clenched his hands.

As no co-respondent had been named in the complaint, the testimony was stricken out, but it had been spoken and had poisoned the public mind as well as that of the jury. Elbert made an eloquent plea, but a verdict was brought in for the plaintiff. It was evident that Scroggins had been bought up, and his envious enmity against the chum of his childhood had found full vent.

"Elbert is so stuck up with city airs he don't know me down at his office. Guess he'll find out a country jay knows a thing or two after all," whispered Peter, defiantly, on leaving the room

It was a shock to Elbert and the defeat he felt very keenly, more especially because it was occasioned by a betrayal on the part of his own witness.

"The jury and witnesses were tampered with. I'll see to this," whispered Bart. "Get a new trial, and we'll show them a trick or two yet."

The prosecution had not calculated upon a stubborn resistance, thinking the wife would meekly submit to avoid further scandal. Bart, in his easy way, approached Housle's attorneys when court adjourned.

"You fellows are going to get into trouble. I am

onto the whole deal. We had some friends on that jury too. It was a dastardly trick to beat the boy."

They knew Bart Waldie; they also knew that he did not indulge in idle threats.

"Well, suppose we drop the suit, as there is nothing in it, and you drop it," suggested the elder attorney.

"Well, there's a red-hot poker waiting for you fellows if you try any more of this on the new trial," said Bart conclusively.

The new trial was granted, and Housle's attorneys seemed to fear an explosion with Waldie's searching black eyes upon them, and they made no such fight as at the former trial, and the result was the wife was fully vindicated.

Peter Scroggins mysteriously disappeared a few days before the second trial, and never appeared in Poplarville again or it might have been unhealthy for him. To reflect upon a pure woman's character aroused the old pioneer spirit of lynch law in Iowa.

This first case in his law career opened to Elbert the book of human nature, and he found in it the real study of life as well as of his profession.

"Trust no one," said Bart, "unless you have a strong rope on him. That's my rule in politics."

Of course the trial made a breach between Elbert and Ned's sister, Kittie, but there was little regret felt on his part.

"Bad brothers sometimes have good sisters, but I'll keep out of the family," thought Elbert, as he smoked and meditated over the dramatic incidents of his first trial.

CHAPTER X.

"By the pricking of my thumbs,
Something wicked this way comes,
Open, locks,
Whoever knocks!"
—Shakespeare.

The peculiarly mingled victory and defeat in the divorce case of Housle vs. Housle brought Elbert forward as one of the promising young lawyers of Chicago. Bart and his wife were naturally quite proud of him, and he continued to grow in prominence in his chosen profession. While Bart continued to prosper in his business and achieved success in his political ambitions, it was evident that in attaining his political aspirations, husband and wife were drifting apart. Agnes suffered in silence as night carousals and political conferences kept Bart away from home days and nights at a time, and Elbert was quick to notice it. He felt like speaking of it in order to avert what seemed to him to be a calamity that would surely result from the present course of proceedings. But the most intimate friends often find some matters too delicate to mention to one another, and to remonstrate with generous, good-hearted Bart seemed more than he could do.

Bart and Mrs. Waldie had made lonely evenings happy for the young man and kept him free from the usual temptations of the city, and his high ideals remained

untainted. With the exception of too much claret
at a banquet at Hinsley's one night his conscience was
clear, and he remembered that night as the occasion
when he had feathers on his feet.

Bart was in the midst of a heated municipal campaign, and Elbert had planned to spend an evening
at their home when a note arrived from McCutcheon,
and it was soon followed by that personage himself—
a tall, angular, smooth-faced man who called himself
a speculator.

"Got your note just now; I was arguing with Ainsworth here about our engagements this evening," said
Bart to McCutcheon, as he was shown in.

"Young fellow, you want to remember who gave you
the glad-hand last fall. You're owned by Boss
Waldie; I give it to you straight," said McCutcheon,
under his breath, to Elbert.

"Never," said Elbert, jumping up excitedly, "he is
my friend but he does not own me; no one save my
conscience owns me."

"Bart, the young fellow feels his oats; the legislature is too high for him," said McCutcheon, grimly.

"There, McCutcheon, that will do," cried Bart;
"Ainsworth is all right, only raised a little differently."

"Yes, gentlemen, raised at my mother's knee; and
I pray the time will come when I shall see a campaign
conducted on principle," retorted Elbert, hotly.

"In our ward it is principal—and interest, office and
boodle, bleed the candidate, sugar the boys and feed
yourself, eh, Bart?" said McCutcheon, with a sardonic
grin.

"Yes, there is no such word as principle in practical politics," he replied.

"I just dropped in for that check you know," continued McCutcheon. "The salary list for the city hall; dead men's row. Flip us your fist and I'll be off.

"We must cut down those dummies, Jimmy."

"Cut nothing; you stick to your word, Bart."

Agnes entered just then. It annoyed Bart, but he introduced McCutcheon politely.

"Mrs. Waldie, Mr. McCutcheon."

"Good afternoon, sir. Bart, when are you coming? I haven't seen you all day."

"Well, ma'am, we have got a whole layout on the cloth for this evening. No telling when we can get back," said McCutcheon.

"Oh, Bart, out again to-night!" said Agnes, but Bart paid no attention to her as she left the room, and went on:

"Schledgmilch is here. Don't go, McCutcheon, till we see how his ward stands. Ah, Schledgmilch, how are you this afternoon?"

Schledgmilch, a very fleshy, pompous man, came into the room.

"Goo' afternoon, efferybody."

"How is the German snarl?" inquired Bart, quickly.

"Off color. No Sherman on the ticket and twenty good saloons in the ward. What vay is dat to do beezness?"

"What do you hear about Turner?" asked Bart.

"Dat's it, dat's it, dynamite and pepper crackers! Dat's the milk in the shestnut. He has the evidence.

I had the tip. Five fellows will swear that we are boodlers of the first water."

This rather astonished Bart and McCutcheon, but Elbert. engaged with his papers, had not apparently taken any notice of the conversation.

"And you had it straight?" asked Bart.

"As straight as we three are crooked," said Schledgmilch.

"Elbert, get the papers ready; I'll spike that young whelp." He's in a glass house himself. Rush the case right through. We'll show old Turner's son that we can squeeze as well as he could with his street cars. Young Turner's mouth must be stopped."

"But, Bart, is this honest?" interposed Elbert.

"Honest be damned! Fight fire with fire; that ward must be carried no matter what it costs. Turner's blood if necessary," replied Bart, heatedly.

"Yes, he's shelling out the money like corn, and some of our boys wink the other eye," broke in McCutcheon.

"Stop Turner's money, put a few fellows on the pay roll and do something for Schneider and we're all right, O. K. up to date. don't it?" said Schledgmilch, as if he had it all settled.

"Will five hundred fix you?" said Bart.

"Beautiful! mid the goose out of sight—of Turner."

"Very well, I'll meet you all at Hinsley's at eight sharp, a .bottle on the quiet, and then to business. Mac, stop in and tell Kinsley I want a private room for six and a small supper—now get out, for I'm very busy."

"Bart, you vas a daisy!" said Schledgmilch.

"I stick by my friends," echoed Bart, as they left.

"Elbert, got that mail all checked up?" continued Bart. "Well, here's my appointment from Washington."

Elbert took it up, read it, and congratulated Bart sincerely. "Now you can pay off old scores without feeling it, Bart." And Bart looked significantly wise and satisfied.

"You've got just a half hour," said Bart, looking at his watch. "Run down and see that something's in the papers to-night; just a line you know: 'The eminent Bart Waldie, the people's favorite, now U. S. Marshal, confidence in his integrity.' Say half a dozen lines."

"It's pretty late, but I'll try," said Elbert, leaving hurriedly as Agnes came into the room.

"Elbert and all gone. I'm glad to have my husband five minutes to myself," she said, putting her arms about Bart's neck as he was seated at his desk looking over papers and schedules.

"There, there, Agnes," he said, putting her off, "don't you see how busy I am?"

"Do we drive this afternoon?"

"Well, hardly, with all I have to do. Have dinner sharp at six, as I've got to be down town at eight."

"Two months married and my husband is lost in the wild game of politics," thought Agnes, leaving the room.

CHAPTER XI.

"Conscience has no more to do with gallantry than it has
with politics."
                —The Duenna, Richard Brinsley Sheridan.

No sooner had Agnes left the room then Bart began
to feel a tinge of remorse over the manner in which
he had treated her. He tried to soothe his feelings
by unstinted generosity in making presents to her old
friends at Poplarville. Through Agnes and Elbert,
and Uncle Jasper, who had known Bart's parents at
Mt. Ariel, Dr. Buzzer, the judge, Mary Jane and all
the residents of Poplarville seemed to Bart like old
friends although he never had seen some of them. He
dreamed of a happy vacation sometime at Poplarville.

As he sat at his desk he reflected: "It is pleasant to
do a kind act; I love the dear old village and all its people. The life of those simple country homes
and country people communing with nature, with a
childlike trust in the future, is preferable to the fever-
ish, pushing, pulse-throbbing existence I spend in
the city. For what? Daily bread, no more."

His reverie was broken by the maid announcing:
"A rough woman insists on seeing you, sir. Mrs.
Waldie is upstairs or I would call her."

She was followed close by Paulina, who hissed in a
vicious way,

"It is better not—it make a mischief—perhaps."

"Well, what is it?" said Bart, with a yawn.

"Ah, what is it not, Naomi?"

"There, that will do, don't speak so loud; you promised never to come here again."

"Ah, that was before—"

"Before what?"

"The fraulein came from the village—the fraulein I say—not the frau."

"You can't frighten any more money out of me."

"No? Who win the love of fraulein; shall I say where? Bah!"

"Our affairs were closed two years ago."

"No!"

"For two years I have tried to lead an honest and honorable life and now you come to make demands upon me; the past is dead and buried."

"No, the sting dies not; my daughter, the frau, she live; the child, your child, he live. The past? No, not dead."

"Paulina, let's talk business."

"It is good, business is good—" said Paulina, sitting on the sofa.

"You know I never married Naomi; you also know she has a monthly allowance from me; that she is in New York, where I expect her to stay."

"Ah, perhaps."

"And for you—well, you remember the bargain."

"The Herr Waldie is rich, influential—Paulina is poor; my son-in-law is a gentleman."

"Your son-in-law?"

"I will sell his picture—as an old rag," she hissed

as she pulled out the faded photograph she had taken
from "Snakes" at Poplarville.

"Where did you get this?"

"Five hundred dollars for silence."

"Why I gave this to—"

The sentence was broken by Agnes appearing at
the door.

"Why, Paulina, when did you leave Poplarville and
how were the folks; what are you doing in the city?"
said Agnes, all in a breath.

"Poplarville," uttered Bart, in a startled way.

"I know not; time is a mystery; wife, children, all,"
responded Paulina, with a vacant sigh.

"Now you must be tired.   I want you to do up two
skirts for me.   And remain for tea," said Agnes, as she
left the room.

"You are in the thirteenth ward," continued Bart.
"Go back to your old work; here's $20 for to-night;
meet me at the old place."

"And Naomi and the child?"

"No matter about that; go before my wife returns."

"The fraulein—"

"I said my wife."

"It is final," said Paulina, with a nasal grunt. "To-
night positive?"

"Yes, to-night.   Come, I'll see you out.   Keep
your mouth closed."

When she had gone Bart breathed easier.   But he
had hardly been seated when the door bell rang and
Schledgmilch and McCutcheon were shown in.

"Have you seen the evening paper, Bart?   Let us

congratulate you. 'Our distinguished Bart,' there it is," said Schledgmilch, showing him an article in a newspaper. Now you go for Tony and blister him."

"Shake, pard; now you can give us the spots. The boys are all shaking over this boodle sensation," said McCutcheon, with a knowing wink.

"You two have got nerve, haven't you?" said Bart, rising. "Everything is working all right; there is just enough of a sensation over Tony's arrest to absorb the boodle sensation. Elbert will pickle that young monkey, and you two keep the boys in line and the affair will soon blow over."

"Like a zummer zephyr," ejaculated the happy German.

"Oh, we are always ready to do the square thing," said McCutcheon, taking a seat.

"The ladies are coming, keep—"

Bart did not finish his sentence; it was Mrs. Daniels who swept in like a puffy squall.

"I told you the nomination would be made; so glad," was her cordial greeting to Bart.

"Gentlemen, Mrs. Daniels of Washington," said Bart, introducing her.

"Get on to the swell outfit; fifty dollar bonnet and trimming to match—Washington pays," said Schledgmilch to McCutcheon, under his breath.

"She knows her biz," responded McCutcheon. "Never stacked the cards, O, no. Let's mosy, Gottleib."

"We are sorry to expel ourselves, Mrs. Daniels," said Schledgmilch, starting towards the door; "we

just blew in to say to the boss, 'you do yourself prou !'
—evnin."

The two backed out of the room bowing profusely,
and when they were alone, Mrs. Daniels at once assumed a business-like air and opened the conversation
directly to the point.

"Now, Mr. Waldie, I must take the midnight train
for Washington; I was so in hopes of seeing Mr. Ainsworth before I left; but we seem to have missed each
other all day."

"I am expecting him every minute."

"So glad; well, you will give me your check for
$3,000 of course."

"$2,000 I thought?"

"Yes, $2,000 and expenses."

"Suppose I write you to-morrow."

"That would hardly do; your check should be made
out to bearer. But there! I was telling you something you of course know yourself. You have doubt-
less given checks to bearer before," she said with an
arch and knowing look.

"Certainly; of course," responded Bart, rather net-
tled.

"Oh, by the way, Mr. Waldie, I had last night a fel-
low-passenger in the sleeper from New York. She
was a lovely young creature. Now I remember she
moaned and tossed all night, crying, 'Bart, Bart, you
will not desert me.' I wormed out of her that she
thought she was married to Bart, but wasn't, you
know—mock ceremony and all that sort of thing, on

the west side, some five years ago. But then Bart is such a common name you know."

"Yes, yes, yes, yes," responded Bart, nervously.

"Perhaps you better give me the check before I go."

"Yes, I think so."

"Senator Forthwith will use his influence in your behalf, and we shall always be friends of course."

"Of course," said Bart, writing out a check.

"Kindly present my regards to Mrs. Waldie," said Mrs. Daniels, coolly folding the check. "Oh, don't disturb her; good-night; many thanks; so glad to meet you; au revoir."

As she started to go through the door she met Elbert.

"You naughty fellow, to dodge me all day—well there—I will see you in Springfield next week unless you come to Washington," said Mrs. Daniels, as she swept out of the room.

"Whew!" said Bart, sinking into his chair. "Elbert, is everything done in the Tony Turner case? You made the arrests this morning?"

"Yes, he was arrested, but the case will likely be put off for some time. Bart, is this invoking the law for private revenge the right thing to do?

"My dear fellow, that is what the law is for," said Bart, with a smile. "Tony Turner seeks to ruin us with that boodle charge. He is guilty of bribery. Now let him take his medicine in just retaliation. If all cases of bribery were prosecuted there would be fewer politicians at large. No; Turner invited this ruin upon himself when he crossed the path of Boss Bart."

CHAPTER XII.

"Then fly betimes, for only they
Conquer love who run away."
          —Old English Song, Thomas Carew.

Through his political associations, Elbert had obtained a few large retainers from corporations. They found him a trusty man, and he modified his radical views of earlier life somewhat as his success advanced. And yet he realized that most of his good fortune came directly through the kind efforts of friends. He was appreciative, and it is always a delight to do a favor and receive a full measure of gratitude in return, and he calculated on gratitude not only as a matter of principle, but of policy, believing that full appreciation of one favor brings other favors.

Elbert had gone on a business trip to the Pacific coast for a corporation and was now on his way home. While in the diner on the overland limited, he fell into conversation with a typical commercial man. Rotund, loud-laughing, hale fellow, always ready with a joke or a story and thoroughly posted on current news and politics was this knight of the grip, and yet, like most other human beings, he possessed a hobby. Always generous and noble hearted.

"Have you ever read Ingersoll?" he asked of Elbert.

"No, but I have heard him lecture—a very fine talker."

"And a thinker, too," responded the commercial man. "There's a man with a mission. He is delivering humanity from the fetich of religious fanaticism and these haggling old hypocrites called preachers."

"Oh, I think you are too severe," said Elbert, jokingly.

"Not at all. I've got enough of 'em. I was raised under the blue laws, but my children, Paine and Voltaire, will never go through the horrors of Sunday schools with their—"

"Hold on; you ought to allow the rest of humanity some comfort. Life is all a delusion more or less, and while I am not a church member I have profound respect for the Bible, and—"

"Respect? Stuff! That book is a pack of vicious lies, a collection of myths. You know the age of reason repels such a gorgeous nightmare, and only the old women idiots—

"That's enough, old man," said Elbert, warmly, rising, "I've a mother; she has a religion, and when she taught me my prayers she taught me to love her. Man, with all your reason you've lost your heart. Give me the simple faith of my mother, and don't take from her in her tottering old age the comfort and serenity of her faith. My God, man, haven't you got a mother?"

"Oh, yes, but you are not old enough to see through these illusions and look upon religion dispassionately, without mawkish sentiment. The hypocrisy concealed in the guise of religion is repellant to any honest man, and if my mother was so foolish—"

"Honest? And yet you would steal away your

mother's religion! Come, old fellow, I don't want to quarrel; let us drop the subject."

Elbert had not noticed particularly the other occupants of the car. An attractive young lady, with rich, black eyes and expressive dimples, had listened attentively to the dramatic conversation, and the eloquent plea of Elbert for his mother's religion. Allie Chatsworth's own mother had died at the old home in Iowa a few months previous, and Elbert's words met with a sympathetic endorsement.

The traveling man went out, and left Elbert to finish his meal in silence. He was about to fold his napkin and follow, when the young lady came toward him and stopped.

"Don't think me rude, sir; but such a mother deserves a noble son. I had a mother—" and she stopped suddenly as tears gathered in her eyes.

"Thank you. Our mothers ought to be our religion," he said warmly.

There was nothing strange in this budding acquaintanceship. The two seemed to drift into conversation. They went back to their car, and Elbert found her a charming companion and talked as long as he thought proper without seeming too assiduous or forward in his attentions.

Elbert found the commercial man in the smoking room entertaining his companions with vile stories and reviling religion. A few words were enough and he went without smoking rather than be irritated by such viciousness. He went back to his seat and gazed out of the window; he tried to sleep and read, anything to while away the leaden moments; but his eyes would unconsciously wander over the top of the Pullman seat in time to catch a glance of two dark eyes innocently looking that way on some pretext or other. Finally he threw off restraint and approached her seat.

"If you don't mind, I am going to talk with you. These long rides are very tedious," he said.

"Perhaps you'll find talking with me more so," she said modestly, as she made a place for him beside her.

He leaned back, tipping his hat over his eyes, and started in to tell his whole life's history, giving it a heroic tinge. Without any real, defined purpose he played upon mother love, music and a fancy tale of disappointed love to touch the very tendrils of a young girl's heart. He even assumed the sad ways of a genius and his dainty fairy love romance was really interesting. After he had allowed full play to his imagination, he turned about to catch a glance of his companion and found her even prettier and more interesting than he had imagined.

"Where do you reside, if I may not be presumptuous in asking?

"At Mauston, Iowa."

"Why, that's only eight miles from Poplarville, my home, and you kept quiet all this time while I was spinning these fancy yarns."

"I enjoyed them," she said, smiling.

"I must candidly confess that there are trifling bits

of imagination in my story that would convict me of prevarication if you knew the truth."

"Don't mind it, I'm not going to be severe with you; but I've met very few people from Poplarville, having been away to school for some years, and it seems so good to meet some one from home," she said, with a spirit of sweet candor in her eyes.

Elbert continued the conversation as most young men of the day would by talking intensely of himself, his hopes and ambitions and ideas. Shortly before they were to part he saw her valise marked, "Mrs. M. H."

Great heavens! he thought; was she married? Well, she had been truly modest and only an agreeable traveling companion after all. But there was something that troubled him in the thought that she was married.

"Are you—you—you—mar—or that is—have you a —a—umbrel—that is—a card? May I call and see you—that is—" mumbled Elbert, feeling himself grow very foolish.

"Certainly, here's my card. Do come and see us when you are at Poplarville," she said with her sweetest smile.

He stopped and looked at the card. "Alice Chatsworth," he read aloud.

"Pretty name," he ventured.

"You like it?"

"Yes, that is—"

"Good-bye," she said, holding out her hand.

"Good—good—can I be of any service? Can I be of any service?"

Elbert rushed out without waiting for an answer, poking his umbrella into grumbling passengers and hurrying as if some one were pursuing him. When he had gone some distance he stopped short and said aloud to himself:

"Say, I'm a fool! Who is this young girl that should make such a dunce of me? I'll go right back and just let her know that I don't care a—"

He went back, but she had gone and he looked in vain for his traveling companion about the station.

"I must see her again to explain myself, anyhow. What an awkward fool she must think me," he reflected.

Just then Cupid winked.

CHAPTER XIII.

"Love took up the Harp of Life,
And smote on all the chords with might."
—Locksley Hall, Tennyson.

It was a favorite practice which Elbert had deduced from his text book on Human Nature to stake out, in fancy, his ambition, and then talk of it as an accomplished fact, depending on pride and honor to impel its achievement. He had a quick perception of humanity and made a close study of human nature. He noted how certain traits were grouped together in certain individuals and how similar characteristics resulted from similar environments; in fact, he made a personal dissection of every acquaintance until he had them classified as accurately as he would plants in botany. Similar impulses he conceived as belonging only to specific types leading to certain well-defined emotions.

But there was one character that puzzled him in spite of his research. His philosophic rules all seemed awry in one particular instance; he could not fathom Allie Chatsworth. Was she a sweet little winsome girl? Yes. Was she a coquette, or why had she disdained to answer his letter? He began to lose interest and ambition in his work.

"I must see her and explain it myself, personally,"

he said one day to Mrs. Waldie, in whom he had confided as to a sister.

"And you think of paying her attentions?"

"No, I am not in love. I simply want to explain my actions—they make me appear so stupid."

"Not altogether without reason, Elbert. But go and see your mother."

"Then Miss Chatsworth will think I have come as a pretense to see her."

"Well, Elbert, that is no crime."

Elbert left for Poplarville that night, and the next morning he walked up the old road shaded with poplars to the corner, shaking hands with old friends. He felt himself quite a personage in the community since he had won the famous Housle divorce case, and he unconsciously sought by wearing gloves, new style collar, and assuming a citified walk to impress his growing importance.

"Knew you would do it; always said so," said Dr. Buzzer. "There's nothing like giving a young man a chance, by ginger," and the doctor blew his nose in the familiar old way as if to accentuate the remark to the group of admiring friends who had gathered to greet Elbert about Jasper's cobbler shop.

"It is good to be home again and breathe the pure air of Poplarville freed from the stuffiness of the city," said Elbert.

"'Um! 'Pears to me you don't walk just as you used to; you land more on your heel than on the sole of your foot," said Jasper, looking over his spectacles at Elbert.

"It is the city pavement, Uncle," responded Elbert, with a laugh.

"And a lawyer's consciousness of the uprightness of his profession," interposed the judge.

"Ah! suppose so; country fellow shuffles, city fellow pegs. I see Abner coming down the road and his weather boots not done. Put your foot up here and let me see. Just as I thought. Land o' Goshen, sole sound, and heels need tapping."

"Welcome back, my boy," said the judge; "how do you like the city? You left us when quite young, hence your impressions should be vivid. Good morning, Miss Toots."

Mary Jane could hold back no longer to get a good look at Elbert.

"Too much sewage, Judge, and not enough sweetness and light," continued Elbert, after greeting Mary Jane heartily. "Well, 'Snakes,' how are you?"

"Mother's dead, mother's dead; didn't see her in the city, did you?"

"No, 'Snakes'."

"All right; I'll just go and talk to mother—mother's dead, you know," she said as she sat by an imaginary grave of sand near the hous

"Abner Tomer says Agnes' husband knows about 'Snakes'; did you hear anything about it?" inquired Mary Jane of Elbert in almost a whisper, with her usual keen appetite for gossip.

All this was in the balmy month of May when every spot in the universe seems in harmony with dreams of budding love. There is something in the virgin fragrance of springtime that generates a cheerful and happy spirit. Elbert did not long remain at the shop and was soon driving past the rich farms on each side of the typical Iowa highway to the Chatsworth place. He was happy, and merrily whistled the tunes he used to whistle when a boy. Each one of the farms he remembered; this was the old Edwards place; here was Beany Brown's lower farm; here Bobby Kenster's old stone house, now fallen, in ruins. As the farmers passed him on their way to the corners he would recall their names and titles in saluting, although they had not been spoken to or thought of by him in the years he had been away. The walnut grove, the old deserted stone quarry, the forbidden thicket, where in spite of warning notices the choice May apples were gathered on the banks of the creek. All these bright memories of childhood; and the reflection came to him, Why had he left them all for the ambitious life in Chicago? He inquired with some timidity as to where the Chatsworth place was located. It seemed peculiar to use that name so freely. On a hill surrounded by an evergreen grove on one side and an orchard on the other was a white farm house, close by, a large red barn and a village of corn-cribs. The white house, with its green shutters and foreground of foliage, made a pretty rural picture. The front garden and veranda were scrupulously neat and had the appearance of not having been used except upon special occasions. As he drove up to the house a typical Iowa farmer came out to meet him. A large man with wiry red chin whiskers, and a good-natured smile playing upon his countenance. There was an awkward pause.

"Is Miss Chatsworth at home?"

"I reckon so. Won't you put up and come in?"

This rather relieved Elbert of his embarrassment, and the farmer called out, with a twinkle in his eye: "Jim, better put up the team and give 'em a feed, as they are likely to——"

"Is Miss Chatsworth inside?" said Elbert, striving to check further embarrassing remarks.

"I reckon she's in the dairy looking after the butter, but I'll call her."

Elbert was ushered into the dark parlor which had the air of disuse. The haircloth furniture, the mahogany what-not, the marble top center table, the old and rich Brussels carpet, the square piano upon which were piled the portfolios of music, the embroidered motto over the door, "God Bless Our Home," all indicated a prosperous farmer's home, even if somewhat out of date.

There was a movement at the door and a bright face and dancing eyes appeared which looked quite familiar. He approached hurriedly.

"Ah!" he said.

"Oh!" she echoed.

"I thought it was Miss Chatsworth," he said, with some embarrassment.

"No; I am her sister. Allie is not at home; she will return soon. Won't you remain?" said the owner of the bright eyes, motioning to the same chair from which he had just risen.

"Thank you; if you don't mind I will wait," said Elbert, settling back rather shyly.

"Are you Mr.—Mr.—of Chicago?"

"Ainsworth.   Ainsworth of Chicago."

"Oh, yes; Allie has spoken of you so often, and she will be delighted to see you.   Now, I was busy in the dairy.   Will you excuse me a minute?"

She returned a few moments later and found Elbert studying a large crayon portrait over the piano.

"That is mamma, and we do not use this room much since she died," she said with sweet and tender emotion.

She kept on busily chatting, and Elbert was charmingly entertained.

"Veo is my name," she said naively to him.   "They call Allie, Miss Chatsworth; she's older than I am." And the eyes so much like her sister's looked up at him innocently.

They enjoyed the afternoon together and Allie did not arrive home until late.   She was very much surprised to see Elbert and appeared embarrassed, but with a woman's tact she tried to be entertaining.   At last she had to confess that she was to "have company" that evening.

"I am so sorry, Mr. Ainsworth; I want to see you so much.   You will remain a day or so and could call——"

"Yes, do," broke in Veo in her girlish way.   "We can have a good time, Mr. Ainsworth."

He was vexed, and yet who could be blamed.   He caught a glance of Veo's bright little smile and said:

"Yes, I'll call again if you'll take care of me."

"Oh, I'll do that. Come, let us go down and see the flowers," said Veo, enthusiastically.

Allie remained in the parlor to entertain the company that evening. She was evidently the lady of the family and had a large retinue of admirers.

Veo related to Elbert her experiences at a distant seminary. "Papa wants me to be a scholar, but I love the dear old farm best. I am so sorry Allie couldn't see you to-night. You must be lonesome."

It was an honest expression of sympathy, but Elbert winced. Then he began to talk of himself in the old strain, and she admired him.

"I love nature," he continued; "the flowers, the birds, and the old trees at home seem like dear old friends."

"Well, that is very pretty talk; but why aren't you a farmer, then?" she asked.

"But I am ambitious to rise in the world."

"Oh, yes," she answered with innocent admiration.

The acquaintanceship progressed famously, and the next day he spent with Allie in the house playing and singing at the piano, and inspecting together the likenesses of all the relatives near and distant from the well-worn plush photograph album. He started to explain his strange procedure at the parting at the railway station and then changed his mind. The next day in leaving, Veo and Allie both asked him to come again, but his first ideal had fallen. Galatea had spoken, but the living marble was not what he had expected.

"I'm muddled," he mused, as he drove home between the willow hedges and over rickety culverts.

Elbert's stay at Poplarville was prolonged beyond his intentions, and his frequent drives into the country occasioned more or less gossip in the village. He was almost a daily caller at the Chatsworth farm and the old farmer was quite favorably impressed with that "city chap." "He'll probably make a match with Allie," was his reflection.

Like all parents he was blind. It was little Veo who held Elbert captive. She gave him unconsciously that pure, wholesome, trusting, confiding friendship, which man most cherishes. They had many long walks and talks together.

"Veo, we never seem to get through talking," said Elbert on the day before leaving. They had wandered down the lane near the old tree at the corner, which was always deserted early in the evening.

"I know it. Oh, I've had such a happy time since you came. But then you came to see—to—to see Allie?"

"Yes, and I found you."

"But who is that fellow Bainsley who is so assiduous in his attentions to Allie?"

"Oh, he's our Sunday-school superintendent," replied Veo.

"A Sunday-school teacher eh? Well, my opinion of Sunday-school men is that they are decidedly egotistical. They are often cranky striplings with sad faces, attempting to teach children the most sacred things of life."

"Well, who else could we secure? They are earnest

and sincere in the effort to do good, and you mustn't feel jealous of Mr. Bainsley. He and Allie only——"

"Bah! Church work is often done for social effect and standing. I sometimes think I am almost a skeptic in religion, although I never could bring myself to revile the faith of my mother, and yet I feel that there is something wrong somewhere."

"Perhaps it is in you," she said.

Here Elbert was again a victim of the desire to bring himself before Veo in a heroic attitude and awaken her sympathy.

"Anyhow, I do not fancy the goody Sunday-school men of 'the day."

"Oh, Mr. Ainsworth, don't let your prejudice destroy a simple faith in Jesus. Dogmas and creeds may be conflicting, but Jesus is real to me."

"Well, it's hard to believe all these things after one has had a broad knowledge of the world. It seems incongruous."

"Oh, don't talk that way, Mr. Ainsworth; it cuts me to the heart," said Veo, pleadingly.

They were sitting on the old tree that had fallen and had been converted into a rustic seat. The deepened twilight had crept upon them and the plaintive chirp of the thrush broke the solitude.

"You are a noble little girl, Veo—"

"Mr. Ainsworth, let me pray for you to-night. I know you have a kind and noble heart, and I want you to be a—a Christian.

Her deep liquid eyes stirred him with the expression

of a kindred soul in their sincerity. But her cheek
paled and her eyes dropped under his gaze.

"Since mamma died I have had no one to talk to
like you," she said.

He moved closer and she looked up at him again
with that deep, soulful glance, and impulsively he
placed his hands on her shoulders, looking deep into
her eyes.

"Veo, do you know what love means?"

She did not answer, but the very repression of
words seemed to reflect the mingled hope and fear in
her heart.

"Veo, Veo," he whispered, drawing her to him.

She dropped back like a tired child, and bending
over her he looked into the depths of those eyes which
spoke the truth her honest heart could not conceal.
The chasing shadows played upon her cheeks and he
leaned over her as she lay upon his arm.

"Veo, Veo," he repeated softly, in tones that could
not be misunderstood. It was love's sweetest cadence.

"I trust you, Elbert."

For some minutes they sat looking deep into each
other's souls. It was a soul communion—pure love—a
welding of the destiny of two lives by a single spark.

"Veo, my own love!—my life!"

"Oh, how happy mamma would be to know you,
Elbert. Elbert, let me pray, I am so happy."

She knelt and turned her eyes toward heaven with
her arm upon Elbert. It was an angelic picture. Her
beautiful black hair had fallen down on her shoulders

and again she turned to him in that simple trusting way.

"Elbert, can you always love a little girl like me?"

"Always, my little Veo," he said, drawing her closer.

"Then you'll love Jesus, too; I know you will, because he has been so kind to me."

Two lives were knit together in that moment and to Elbert it was the supreme hour of his life.

"Veo! All my own Veo!"

"Yes, Elbert, all yours."

"Little girl, you do not know all the wickedness of the world and of men. Are you willing to leave the old farm?"

"Anywhere, Elbert; I trust you. Mamma has blessed her little girl."

There were a few tears which seemed like a gentle baptism of heavenly dew. Hardly knowing it, Elbert had drifted to his fate, and he was happy.

CHAPTER XIV.

"An attempt to bribe, though unsuccessful, has been holden to be criminal."   —Bouvier.

It was all like a dream to Elbert as he walked back to Poplarville. He told his mother of his engagement just before leaving for Chicago, and she gravely asked him, "Are you sure she is the right one, Elbert?"

"Quite sure, mother. She has a soul. Veo is my ideal of trusting and pure womanhood, and, mother, no words carried the message of love between us. I feel a purer and nobler man for having won such a love, and you will be a mother to her and make her happy, I know. Good-bye."

"Good-bye, my boy. God bless you."

Elbert had been in Chicago scarcely an hour before he was at Waldie's and had told the story. They were of course very much pleased, and Mrs. Waldie asked: "You are sure you love her, Elbert?"

"Why are you women so skeptical? Cannot the heart speak plainer than mere words?"

"All right, Elbert; I only wanted you to make no mistake, for destiny is often decided when troth is plighted."

"So that's where you've been all this time, is it?" broke in Bart, looking up from his paper. "Well, we all catch it at one time or another. But they have been raising the deuce in politics since you left, and I'm just now mapping out plans for a fall campaign."

"What seems to be the matter?" asked Elbert.

"Well, you know political success is not gained without making enemies. Your acceptance of that corporation fee on that western trip has made it impossible for you to be a candidate."

"But what has that to do with it?" asked Elbert.

"Well," continued Bart, with a shrug and running his fingers through his curly hair, "they say you are a boodler."

Bart was always prepared for emergencies. The opposition papers the next morning charged Bart and Elbert with being boodlers and fit candidates for State's prison.

The friendly papers retaliated by a charge of bribery against Tony Turner, who was still under arrest, the son of a wealthy street railway owner. Tony had made himself particularly obnoxious by heavy contributions to the campaign funds of the opposing party. In fact, they said that if they could kill Tony off that would cut off the sinews of war for the opposition. He was a sort of a cad, and was not particularly popular even among those with whom he was politically identified. There was just enough truth in the charge of bribery to silence his alleged supporters, and the former friends of his days of dissipation one by one deserted him. Turner was a particularly bitter opponent of Bart Waldie, having defeated him in securing several large contracts by financially backing the rival bidders.

The newspapers which had precipitated the boodle and bribery fight dared not stop now for fear of public opinion insisting that Turner's money had silenced them. The agitation grew into a fever of public indignation, and even the judge who granted young Turner bail was censured. The populace were aroused and seemed to want to wreak vengeance on Tom Turner's son.

The lawyers with political ambitions were all afraid to accept a retainer in the case for the defense, and yet it was a case that required a semi-political lawyer. Turner was seen in Elbert's office, and this at once aroused the suspicion of gossips. Later young Turner's mother accompanied him to Elbert's office.

Elbert had been, in local political affrays, Turner's direct political opponent.

"Ainsworth, for God's sake take this case. I am innocent. Here's my mother to plead with you; name your price."

"Yes, Mr. Ainsworth," broke in the mother. "You are too much of a man to stand by and see an innocent boy suffer."

"Madam, I am afraid I shall have to return the same answer I have given your son. I cannot take the case," said Elbert, firmly.

"But why?" pleaded Tony.

"To be perfectly frank, I am already under suspicion. You surely understand my situation. It would make a breach between Bart Waldie, the best friend I ever had, and myself; besides—"

"But this is a case of law, not politics," said the mother.

"Yes, Madam, but you know politics creeps into everything nowadays. It may be well disguised, but it is there."

"Ainsworth, your fee would be more than—"

"Stop! I'm not to be bought. Your millions would not tempt me."

"Yes; but they are killing me—a victim of blackmailers and political plotters. I would not care for myself, but poor mother! It is killing her."

"Mr. Ainsworth, as a lawyer you took an oath, and your honor and duty demands that you do not refuse a retainer offered to further the ends of justice, no matter how it may conflict with political affiliations," said the mother.

"Well, I will think it over and give you an answer to-morrow," said Elbert, going to the door with them.

After they had retired a telegram was handed to Elbert. The language was rather strange for a message; it read: "Dear Elbert—Defend Tony Turner; he is innocent, I know. He spent last summer here and he is a noble fellow. Your Veo."

Tony a rival for Veo's love, and now defend him? Never. This quite convinced Elbert that he should refuse the case, and yet here was an urgent request from his future wife. It was a difficult problem. Should he clear a rival in love, make a breach with Bart, his best friend, destroy his promising political aspirations, all for the sake of a lawyer's fee?

"Well, I'll go and see Mrs. Waldie about it." He

found her in a sad mood and alone, Bart having gone to "set up the pins down town," as he said.

"Elbert, this political life is killing poor Bart," she said.

"I know it, and it is killing us all; I am afraid his prestige is waning, and to be defeated would crush him. He has just ordered three hundred and six barrels of flour distributed in hopes of helping matters."

"But Bart is at heart a generous fellow, politics or no politics," said the wife, feeling a little hurt that anyone should say an ill word of her husband.

Elbert then related the circumstances in reference to the Turner case; also showing her the telegram from Veo. Mrs. Waldie studied a minute and then arose with that queenly flash in her deep blue eyes he remembered so well.

"Do your duty as a man, Elbert, next as a lawyer; but kill political ambition rather than let it cost you your manhood."

"But it will make trouble between Bart and me—"

"It does not matter," she answered; "your manhood is at stake. If that young man is innocent—defend him. That is clearly your duty."

"But supposing Bart—" remonstrated Elbert.

"Trust Bart's generosity. But even if it does create a breach, better that than personal and professional dishonor. Elbert, be a man, brave and true, no matter how precarious the reward may seem."

The decision was made.

The announcement of his decision to Mrs. Turner and her son was delayed several days, owing to a crisis

in the local political situation which kept him away
from his office. Turner and his mother naturally concluded that Elbert's absence was merely an evasion
to indicate a negative answer, and they were discouraged.

Bart Waldie had been busy night and day seeing
that the primaries were all carried for his candidates.
A spasmodic wave of reform worried the machine
manipulators somewhat, but the reformers were dis-
organized and lacked the real spirit of reward which
animated the cohorts of Boss Bart. Waldie had been
busy visiting all of the critical wards in the city during
the day, and a drink of liquor here and there had
almost resulted in intoxication, but his intellect seemed
keener than ever to see the weak points along the
line.

"Elbert, you must see to that ward of Hunkey-
Dorey. Cacklin will have to be renominated for alderman to get him out of Jenkins' way for sheriff."

"Shall I talk to them?"

"No: try and steer Cacklin. He thinks he is an
orator. Cultivate him and he is good for a thousand
in the fall campaign fund."

A glimpse into the caucus methods then in vogue
had disgusted Elbert pretty thoroughly with politics
as a career. Alderman Cacklin and other distinguished
saloon men had looked to Bart for the brains and they
kept the reserves ready to carry any caucus at a moment's notice. The crowd would simply rush into the
place where the caucus was to be held, shouting for
their own chairman, and when he was elected he in

turn recognized only his own men. All this is legal because it is the will of the majority. The influence of the tough element was positive, while that of the better class was negative.

An attempt had been made by a number of respectable citizens in Cacklin's ward to hold a caucus, and Hunkey-Dorey, the renowned plugger, had just completed the work of routing them and securing Cacklin's nomination as alderman. Hunkey-Dorey stood on a billiard table, triumphant in his glory. The room was dense with tobacco smoke and very convenient to Cacklin's saloon in the rear. The newly nominated alderman was escorted in by a committee and after a polite bow and his blushes had subsided he read a piece which had been prepared for him, and the crowd applauded every time he stopped for breath. He said:

"Fellow citizens—Like my illustrious colleague, Dave, I am a good citizen. I wish to say that I am proud that I am a good citizen. There hasn't been a scrap in this ward to-day. No policeman has been called into this convention except to get a cigar. I do not wish to be ambiguous, so I here and now state my platform in words of no uncertain tone. My object if I am again elected shall be to repeal the law prohibiting saloons from remaining open all night. I believe in base hits and competition. Thank you. Will you join me?"

The reserves were not long in joining—in fact that was the exceedingly interesting part of the proceedings.

That night Bart and Elbert were talking over the campaign.

"This is the last time we are going through with this kind of work, my boy. You've been true blue and will not be forgotten."

"Bart, I feel as if it were all wrong."

"Well, we have this material in the sovereign voter— some party will utilize it, and why not us as well as the other fellows?"

"Yes; but I'm through with it now."

"You stay by your friends, and you're all right. We'll get some juicy plums out of this deal. I want you to go to Congress, Elbert, some day. You will be an honor to us."

"It is not unpleasant to contemplate."

"It is a sure thing. You've been too loyal to your friends not to succeed. Political succession grows like everything else. But there are some ugly political complications just now—but then, we'll talk it over to-morrow."

CHAPTER XV.

"I am armed with more than complete steel—
  The justice of my quarrel."
  —"Hero and Leander," Christopher Marlowe.

As Elbert sat on the edge of his bed and reflected
the following morning, he felt that a storm was coming. The longed-for favorable decision was given to
Tony Turner, whom he found awaiting him at his
office. The young man fairly hugged Elbert with joy,
and his worried mother who was with him gave him
a grateful smile which Elbert felt guilty in receiving.
Veo had arrived that day to visit with Agnes, and
Elbert was anxious to get home, as they were preparing for a cosy little dinner, "just we four together,"
as Veo said as she went out to help Agnes prepare
the meal.

"Well, old man, we will have that young monkey
of a Turner pickled, and then we will have smooth
sailing. It's all fixed; you are to steer for the congressional nomination, and if you get it you are certain of an election no matter what happens," said
Bart, settling down with a satisfied air.

"But, Bart, I am to defend Turner," said Elbert.

Defend what? Are you crazy? What are you talking about?" said Bart, getting up excitedly.

"I have accepted a retainer to defend Turner, and—"

"Sold out, and by you! Elbert, my God! Say that you are joking," said Bart, with his eyes flashing.

"It is true," responded Elbert, firmly.

"What, what, defend? Are you crazy, or mad, or jealous, or what?"

"None of these. I am simply doing what appears to me to be right under the circumstances."

"Why boy! right? right? You a traitor, you, to knife me at this critical moment. By God, you young snip, you will find it don't pay."

"Bart, listen; there is a reason."

"Reason be damned; what reason can excuse your treachery? You know Bart Waldie can be a foe as well as a friend."

"Bart, don't lose your head—you have been a father to me. In defending Turner I am simply doing my duty as an attorney; some other lawyer will prosecute your case just as well as I, and perhaps better."

"Don't talk like a ninny; there's some other reason; what is it?"

Veo and Agnes came into the room, having heard the stormy words between the two men.

"Yes, Mr. Waldie, there is another reason. Tony Turner is my cousin," said Veo, coming towards him.

"Oh, that's it?" sneered Bart. "And are you not ashamed to listen to silly women who know nothing of the affairs of the world; how much money did you get?"

"Bart, you are going too far," said Agnes; "Elbert has served you faithfully. He thinks it his duty to appear for Tony now." .

"Stop there; I am master in this house and I don't wish to hear another word from you. As for you, sir, you will find other quarters at once; no traitors in my camp; what's the bribe you got from Turner?"

"Bart Waldie, you are a contemptible liar!" said Elbert, starting toward him with clenched fists.

Veo screamed and Agnes coolly placed herself between the enraged men.

"Now get out; I will teach you a lesson to remember," said Bart, hotly. "I stay by my friends through thick and thin, but my enemies I crush."

"Come, let us be men," implored Elbert.

"Go," hissed Bart, furiously.

"Bart," interposed Agnes.

"You, too, if you say another word," he said, turning to her savagely.

"Oh, Bart," sighed Agnes piteously, as Elbert led the two ladies from the room, without a glance back towards Bart.

When alone Bart took the faded likeness given him by Paulina from his desk.

"Oh, Naomi, Naomi! Oh! God forgive my sins!"

The lull had come after the storm.

* * * * * * *

Veo returned home, and Elbert plunged into the work connected with the trial with all the vigor of youth, and with the feeling that he was in the right, but realizing that it blasted his bright political prospects. The trial was one of the most notable in the city during that year, and the wonderful power of Elbert and his assistant counsel seemed almost super-

human, because they were thoroughly prepared with
strategic points and had unearthed a large amount of
unexpected evidence. The beginning of the trial was
decidedly unfavorable for Turner, but the very oddity
and unexpectedness of every play on the legal chessboard confused the prosecution. The state's attorneys
in their blind semi-political vindictiveness neglected
to take note of the law of reaction.

In his closing plea Elbert said:

"I am here a poor man's son to plead for the rich
man's son."

He reviewed carefully the testimony of the state,
showing that it was thoroughly colored with malice
and concluded with a simple but sincere plea for justice
and humanity, insisting that the angry mob spirit
should not rule. Young Turner sat near by, pale and
excited, the victim of dissipation and now of worry,
feeling deeply a degradation in having his mother's
name dragged into criminal court. Elbert attempted
to shield none of his client's faults, and his earnest and
candid statement as to his own personal connection
with the case was thrilling. He was an orator who
could move men, and felt that the jury was with him.
He had carefully studied each of the twelve men, and
in reality made twelve separate pleas. He played upon
the twelve individuals as upon so many strings of a
harp, and the effect was magical.

"I am right—God knows I am right!" were his
closing words, and they were spoken with an earnestness which thrilled his auditors.

The jury retired and had been out twenty-four hours

without reaching a verdict. This was a surprise, as
the general opinion had prevailed that a verdict of
guilty would be a question of only a few moments'
consideration by the jury, and there were black hints
as to Turner's money "hanging the jury."

The verdict was announced the following afternoon,
when young Turner and his mother had returned to
the court room after a night of terrible suspense, and
in a way it was unexpected.

"Not guilty," spoke the foreman of the jury in solemn tones.

For Elbert it was a great legal victory, but in the
breach with Waldie he suffered the loss of a kind
friend, and it stung him bitterly to be looked upon as
an ingrate.

A fee of five thousand dollars was paid to him, and
yet what was that in comparison with his lost political
honors and Bart Waldie's friendship. In fact the legal
victory virtually destroyed his law practice. Many
of his old clients deserted him, but he still felt that he
was in the right. A little square envelope brought him
a message that he knew would prove that he was
right.

"My own dear Elbert: You noble boy—all for me
you cleared poor Cousin Tony; but I knew he was
innocent. What a relief to his mother. Oh, my noble
knight; how your little Veo loves you! I always
keep the shield of your love bright and shining, like
Elaine, but you will not leave me like Lancelot, will
you, my own darling Elbert? I am so happy and
proud of you. Your own Veo."

"That settles it," reflected Elbert, jumping up. "We'll be married while this fee lasts and not take chances on another." And he wrote and asked for a date for their wedding.

CHAPTER XVI.

"Bring flowers, bring flowers for the bride to wear."
—Mrs. Hemans.

A wedding in Poplarville even in this decade was an interesting event. There was in it just enough of the reflection of city life to give the contrast. In the Chatsworth neighborhood the wedding of Veo and her "city fellow" was looked forward to as the particular event of the year. The preparations were very elaborate. Allie had been married since Elbert's first visit, but it was a wedding that did not attract general interest in the neighborhood, as Allie had been absent so much of recent years that she had rather drifted away from the close affections of the neighbors. But little Veo was endeared because in spite of her seminary culture she still loved the farm and was proud of being a farmer's daughter. She had been the special favorite of her mother, and her simple, outspoken and sympathetic nature was lovable; always happy, her winsome ways made friends of all with whom she came in contact. The women of the neighborhood all joined in the preparations of the wedding feast, which was to be such an one as only farmers' wives could provide.

There was, too, a strained relation between Allie and her husband and Veo and Elbert because of the suppressed feeling by the former that the father would

favor the younger daughter in his will. Mr. Chatsworth was reputed to be well-to-do, and the young
men were looked upon to some extent as heiress hunt-
ers.

Elbert arrived a few days prior to the wedding and
found Veo very busy and very happy.

"Oh, Elbert, I am so glad you've come. My noble
boy! Now you can help me plan. There's ice cream
and fruit and pressed chicken to be looked after, and
I want everything all right for you, my dear."

"But, little one, don't overwork; why all this fuss
for me?"

"Elbert, a girl loves to have a big wedding when
she has such a fine, noble husband as you are; I want
all the neighbors to see you; I am not selfish, and
you like it, don't you, dear?"

"Yes, yes," he answered, with a resigned air.

They were leisurely walking down the old familiar
lane to the corners.

"You are a noble little girl, Veo," said Elbert, trying
to find new phrases in which to express his love.

"And always yours, Elbert."

"Always—and a day."

"Let me have you five minutes all to myself before
the ceremony. You have been gone so long. Everybody will want to talk to you."

"It does seem an age."

"And then you were only back for a day."

"Little girl, are you willing to leave the old farm
for the city?"

"Anywhere, Elbert, with you."

"You little angel."

"Just think, Veo, this is the same spot where we were betrothed a little over a year ago."

"And I do believe that is the same thrush that made her nest then."

"And the same cat-bird that called to us, 'I see you'."

"Every day I have come to the old tree while you were making your way in Chicago, until Uncle Jasper and 'Snakes' have got tired of seeing me."

"Snakes" was coming toward them, muttering: "You back again; come for the funeral, eh? Mother's dead."

"You must not mind 'Snakes,' Elbert; she does not always quite know what she says," said Veo, as Elbert watched "Snakes" sitting by the imaginary grave.

Abner Tomer passed by just then and hailed Veo.

"Your father's looking for you to come, Veo; heaps of things to do before sundown, if you're making to get hitched. How'dy, Elbert."

"How are you, Deacon Tomer. Hope the church has been flourishing," said Elbert, good-naturedly.

"Nothin', nothin' out o' common. There's talk of one of them railroads through our village, so'm told; never want to see one of the darned things; they run on iron."

"This is an age of machinery, Deacon," said Elbert.

"And mother's dead," added "Snakes."

"Darn the women, anyhow," said Abner, seeing "Snakes." "There's that child of Bart's—but that's a long story. Veo, Veo, child, run home; your pap's missing you. Mister City-chap," he continued to El-

bert, "this may be an age of machinery, but I'll be
darned if I want to be buried by machinery. 'Pears
to me your collar's kind of stiff, too; ironed by machinery, so'm told. Paper ones are good enough for
me."

With this declaration he shuffled off up the lane,
whipping the weeds with his cane.

"What are you doing there, pet?" asked Elbert,
turning to Veo.

"Oh, only my daily crumbs for the birds," she said,
as she scattered a handful and the flock of birds fed
upon them in the road near by.

"Sweet girl, you are giving me more than crumbs of
comfort," said Elbert; "our nest will be as peaceful and
homelike as theirs."

"Yes, and filled with as many young ones," cried
out Jasper from inside of the shop where he was at
work. He was afraid the young lovers might get
too much interested. "Don't forget the Bengalese
proverb: 'Love like a creeper withers and dies if it
has nothing to embrace.' The home's the thing to
hold the conscience of your king," he continued, crit-
ically examining his work while he was talking. "Glad
to see you, Elbert, back safe and sound, but we are all
sorry to lose Veo. Now, as Aristotle says, page 24—"
but the lovers had escaped up the road out of hearing.

They had not gone far when they met Mary Jane
bustling down the lane, with a regiment of helpers,
putting the finishing touches to the bridal bower
located under the old tree at the corners.

"Land o' Goshen, you here yet!" said she to Veo.

"Child, come in and get a shawl to put around you, and then run in while I finish getting out the baking."

Veo gave a longing look at Elbert and left to go into the house. For a while all was confusion in the final preparations for the wedding.

"My stars alive! But you folks is the dawdlest passel of people in seven corners. Sundown here—folks a-comin', the elder in sight and nothin' done. Snakes, get in them pies; Simon, put that festoon the other way," fairly screamed Mary Jane to those at work.

"Let me help, Mary Jane," said Shandy, as he started to go off with a pie.

"Put down that pie, Shandy; if it gets into your hands no one else will get a taste of it. That's choice, filled with gooseberry."

It was in the early autumn and it was Veo's fancy to be married under the old tree where their love message had been spoken.

"To me it is a sacred spot, Elbert, and it always brings back such happy memories," she urged when the choice was made.

The ceremony was to occur at twilight in God's own temple to the music of rustling leaves.

At an early hour the local Methodist minister and his family of ten arrived. An elderly man with long beard and smooth upper lip. Later the neighbors came pouring in. The teams were "put up" and everyone prepared for a good time at Veo's wedding. Of course there were many green country boys and girls there who had never been out in society much, and the city fellows with new style collars tried to be particularly at ease and overwhelmingly impressive. The country guests gathered in chairs placed in rows along the walls of the room of Mary Jane's cottage, and sat there as solemnly as at a funeral. A few were courageous enough to peep through the double glass at stereoscopic views; others sat and gazed at the walls and the dangling glass prisms of the hanging lamp. The guests were first ushered into a typical farmhouse chamber, where wraps were removed. The rag carpet of fantastic colors, the valanced drapery about the bed and pitcher with the splasher behind, embroidered with letters inviting to the morning bath, gave an air of sweet home comfort, Mary Jane's ideal.

At the appointed hour the bridal couple came down stairs.

Elbert stately and handsome, but nervous, and Veo blushing and more beautiful than ever, reaching up to her lover's arm, perfect in her radiant happiness.

As they passed by the parlor door the bridal chorus from "Lohengrin" was played on the piano at double quick tempo, with a charming flavor of Wagner in the chords, by reason of the piano being out of tune. The guests remained in the parlor until the bridal party had passed out, and then joined the procession and formed a semi-circle about the bridal bower. The soft twilight seemed to give the scene a weird and solemn aspect, and even Nature mingled congratulations, as scarcely had the words been spoken pronouncing them husband and wife when a shower of autumn leaves fell upon them as a benediction. The elder, in his homely but eloquent prayer, referred to "the sainted mother in heaven," and many eyes moistened as he nearly broke down. They sang the doxology, "Praise God from whom all blessings flow," and that seemed to clear the atmosphere. Then Elder Whoops proclaimed proudly: "Now let me introduce you to Mr. and Mrs. Ainsworth; Elbert, allow me to congratulate you; and Veo, well—I've got to set the fashion," and he kissed her with a hearty smack.

After Farmer Chatsworth came Jasper and the doctor, as they struggled to speak the words of congratulation.

"Now, folks, come right in," said Mary Jane, grand marshal of the day, "the victuals are getting cold. Elder Whoops, lead the way there. Melancthon, you wait until the children are helped. Here, the bride next—that's right—no, go right in; there's room for all."

A young man from the city had gallantly kissed the bride and wished her joy, but the blushing country boys only shook hands and mumbled, "How are ye? Glad to meet ye," scarcely daring to look at Veo, whom their honest, noble hearts worshiped as a queen.

We love to linger in these happy memories of weddings. The feast and music soon loosened the reserve of the country boys and girls, who at first looked upon Elbert as something of a usurper. After the guests had nearly all gone, Elbert and Veo inspected the array of wedding presents. There were quilts and pillow shams, plush albums and splashers by the dozen, knives and forks, spoons, and a formidable array of perfumery bottles, and innumerable trinkets and useful articles for housekeeping equipment.

"So kind of them, Elbert. I love them all, and they love you, my true knight," said Veo, proudly. Just then they were interrupted in their pleasant reveries.

"By gosh, I forgot one thing," said Gee Watkins, just coming up. "The boys sent me up with this. Ha! ha!"

It was a baby carriage, and there was a chorus of titters behind the hedge.

"All right, Gee. Thank you very much," said Veo, pleasantly.

"Good-bye, good-bye, Veo. What will we do at singing-school without you?"

"Oh, you'll find some other girl," said Veo, merrily. "Good-bye."

Before going into the house, Elbert and Veo wandered over to the wedding bower. The candles and the Chinese lanterns had almost burned out.

"Here, Elbert, I gave my life to you," said Veo, solemnly.

"Sweet little one, you are now all my own. Nothing can ever part us," and he drew her to him and again looked into her honest eyes, and repeated softly, as if recalling memories of the happy trysting place, "Veo, Veo."

And the whispering winds through the summits of the trees seemed to echo his words again and again.

CHAPTER XVII.

"We've scotched the snake—not killed it."
                    —Macbeth.

The young couple went directly to Chicago, where
Elbert was going to make a struggle to retrieve his
shattered law practice. They had rented a flat, and
Mrs. Waldie was already there to welcome them and
assisted the young girl wife in fitting up the new home.
She continued her friendship to Elbert in spite of
the breach with Bart, hoping in some way to reconcile
the two men later on. The child wife loved her, and
there were few moments for homesickness with Mrs.
Waldie and Elbert around. The fee of five thousand
dollars was in the bank, and after a few weeks Elbert
called his wife for consultation.

"Veo, I feel the lack of a collegiate education. I
am not equipped to achieve permanent success in the
profession of law, and I am discouraged."

"Oh, no, Elbert, you can study by observation," said
Veo, cheerily. "We can travel and I will take good
care of things. We can study together—only—only—
I don't know much about law."

"Yes, but your little head is chuck full of common
sense, and that is better than law."

The matter was submitted to Mrs. Waldie and she
approved of Veo's plan.

"Travel and intelligent observation will soon cover

all defects, Elbert. Don't give up now. You have only begun."

Veo and Elbert were then at Waldie's house. Agnes had insisted on matters continuing as before. Bart was not at home when they arrived, and they had enjoyed a delightful evening together. They were about to leave when Bart came in. His face was flushed. He saw Agnes and Elbert, but not seeing Veo, he said: "You here? And haven't you any pride? What an honor, Mrs. Waldie, to nurse a viper who has stung us! No wife of mine shall—"

Just then Veo stepped out.

"I am Elbert's wife, sir."

"Beg pardon, Miss, but—but—you don't know," mumbled Bart. "They are all plotting to ruin me. But I'll show them yet that old Bart isn't dead," and he shuffled on upstairs, slamming the door.

"Shall we remain?" asked Elbert, anxiously.

"No; it will be all right," said the plucky but sorrowing wife.

When they had reached home Veo said, "Oh, how I pity her, Elbert. Can't we make her happy some way?"

"I hope so," he replied.

"I wish I knew more, Elbert, so I could talk to you as she does."

"No, pet; you are all right as you are," he replied, lovingly.

This was the first real explosion in Bart Waldie's married life. Matters had been growing desperately worse for him since the estrangement with Elbert.

The young man was more to him than he had ever supposed. He had begun to lean upon Elbert, and now with that support gone the downfall of "Boss Bart" seemed only the question of a very short time, and with it was to come the wreck of his business and health.

A suit for divorce suggested itself to Agnes, but she shrank from making her personal troubles a public matter. There were good grounds for a divorce, but she lived on in patient sorrow, man and wife treating each other almost as strangers. Bart seemed to have lost all manhood; his life was wrecked and his hopes yet unachieved. It was a sad life for Agnes. Wealth and the honors and burdens of social position, and yet no home. A hungry, lonesome wife's heart feeding upon its own bitterness.

The following morning brought no change in the brewing domestic trouble. Husband and wife passed each other in silence. As Bart was about to leave, Agnes inquired: "Bart, why are you so bitter and unrelenting; why not forgive Elbert?"

"Woman, will you hold your tongue; you will drive me mad yet; that young scoundrel has not only wrecked me, but the party as well."

"But, Bart, he followed the dictates of his conscience and did not willingly do wrong."

"He is a Judas; he did not stick by his friends, but sold them out," he retorted as he rushed out from the house in a rage.

A few minutes later Paulina Cracovitz was shown in from the kitchen. Agnes was startled to see her.

"The fraulein has returned; it is good; Herr Waldie is not sick perhaps?"

"No, Paulina; Mr. Waldie is quite well."

"Ah, not sick the heart?"

"Why, no; why should he be?" said Agnes, slightly
disturbed by the impertinent remark.

"Ah, why? Bad man, they are sick in the heart
sometimes; devils, no, never."

"Paulina, what are you hinting at? And why do
you want to see me? Why did you not come back for
the skirts I wanted washed?"

"Ah, Herr Waldie has much work for me to do.
Oh, yes?" muttered Paulina, with a devilish leer.

"For you? Explain yourself, woman."

"Um!" she said with a grunt. "South Clark
Street, State Street, Dearborn Street. Um, 'um, some
women to see; some men money to spend—oh, Paulina know."

"Some women to see; some men; and money to
spend—you?"

"Why not? Herr Waldie is my son-in-law."

"Merciful heaven! What are you saying?"

"The fraulein get crazy," continued Paulina, shaking her head. "She kill Herr Waldie. No, no; he
have not paid the price full. No! No!"

"Tell me what he has done, I command you."

"Command? Ah! I like it."

"Then I entreat you as one woman to another."

"Bah! The fraulein is impatient. He promise—he
break the promise. I break him in this little hand; so!"

"But what has he done?"

"Oh, much; women, women, always women!"

"I will not believe it."

"No? Look at that," she said, handing her a paper.

"Marriage certificate, Bart Waldie, Naomi Thompson; woman, you lie!" cried Agnes, almost beside herself.

"My daughter—his wife."

"I cannot and will not believe it."

"Oh, it is the word from heaven. The sting is deep for both; for you, for me, for both. Go back, tell Herr Waldie he pray through the nose. I will it; I will it."

"You are a scheming, blackmailing gypsy. I will believe nothing against my husband. He is too good, too noble to deceive me. Oh! Bart! Bart!"

"Perhaps you think so. The idiot girl, too, she know a thing."

"Snakes? It is monstrous. Great God! I am crushed!" cried Agnes, sinking into a chair.

"Go, tell him Paulina lives for vengeance. Blood for blood, wife for wife. I will, I will have his heart, his life. Ah, Naomi! My child! His life! My son-in-law! Bah! Paulina lives—," and with the old gypsy oath, shading her eyes as if from the sun with the blade of her dagger, she left the house.

CHAPTER XVIII.

"The use of traveling is to regulate imagination by reality, and instead of thinking how things may be, to see them
as they are."
                                                —Dr. Johnson.

Elbert and his wife left soon after on what Veo
called "our educational observation tour." She was in
high glee and carefully packed each piece of luggage
so that Elbert would have no trouble in searching for
anything. Although she had never traveled much her
housewifely instincts made the most of every emergency for neatness and comfort. Elbert took copious
notes and Veo carefully copied and indexed his work
as they traveled about. They first went to Washington, arriving late in the evening. It was raining, and
the mirrored reflections on the asphalt pavements gave
the city a Parisian aspect. They stopped at the old
National Hotel because that was where Henry Clay,
one of Elbert's heroes, had lived and died. They
were assigned to the corner room on the second floor
where the great compromiser had breathed his last.

"My, but we must expect to see ghosts to-night,
Elbert," said Veo, mysteriously.

"These historical associations are real inspirations,"
he responded with mock bravery.

"Well, I'm not afraid of anything when you're
around, Elbert."

The following days they visited all the points of interest, as thousands of bridal couples before them have done. From the Washington Monument they had a sweeping perspective of the reclaimed Potomac flats, the historic Arlington Heights and Robert Lee's mansion, the Mall, the White House, the Treasury Building and the Capitol. This was Elbert's first visit to the scenes often read of in his school history.

They took the usual routine of tourists. They went into the Capitol with its labyrinth of low-arched passages with a feeling of awe. The whispering galleries, the paintings, the rugged, massive solidity of the stairway, were all impressive. In the House of Representatives, as they looked down from the public gallery there was a continuous buzz which recalled the Chicago Board of Trade or a country caucus. Several set speeches were being delivered, and Veo remarked under breath: "Elbert, you can do better than that; but what funny old cane seat chairs and antiquated school desks," she continued; "a seat in Congress doesn't amount to much, after all, does it, Elbert?"

The Senate with its impressive air of courtesy and dignity was a marked contrast to the House. And here Elbert indulged in an elaborate day dream. In fact, all these scenes were stimulating the political ambition of the young lawyer. In the Supreme Court room what an air of repose and serenity; in their sombre black gowns, the justices personified the idea of a final matured human judgment. Motions were rattled along the bench; whispered conferences of the moment resulted in momentous decisions, and an oc-

casional smile flitted from face to face like a gleam
of sunshine in a dark abyss. The red plush seats for
spectators were filled, but each justice was absorbed
in his work and was entirely oblivious of the visitors.

A few days later it became evident to Elbert that he
must do something to replenish his financial reserve.
Through Bart Waldie he was known to a number of
prominent politicians in Washington, but the more
he saw of Bart's party friends the less he thought of
the party in which he had trained under Waldie. His
father's political beliefs began to take possession of him
again, and like the prodigal son he returned to the
original political fold after talking the matter over
with Veo.

"Elbert, believe what is right. It is surely not a
crime to change political faith."

"Veo, my political faith is changing, but what will
Bart and my old political friends in Chicago think?"

"Why, just let them keep on thinking, Elbert; it
won't hurt them."

That afternoon he was interviewed by a newspaper
friend and his change of conviction was announced
more or less prominently by the opposition papers.
He obtained a conference with a prominent politician
who was then in the zenith of his career as a statesman. Elbert told him briefly his life experience in an
open, candid way.

"You are a brave lad, but you lack thorough acquaintance with the idea of protection which you have
embraced as a political creed. You are impelled per-

haps by impulse—your little wife you speak of—may have—"

"But, sir, it is a matter of honest conviction with me."

"No doubt; but found your beliefs on facts."

"Is a political career advisable for me?" inquired Elbert.

"No, young man; decidedly not. Do you see those gray hairs? Defeated, maligned and chagrined. It is a bitter, unwholesome career. My advice to young lawyers is 'less office holding and more law.' I hope that I am forever through with politics."

"But I feel that I have a mission in the coming campaign, even if without hope of reward, to retrieve the past."

"Well," continued the statesman, "know your subject first, and to clearly comprehend the protective policy you ought to travel abroad and make the study by observation and comparison of existing facts without the intervention of theory. A trip abroad will broaden not only your political but literary comprehension, and do not attempt to go into a political campaign without being fully equipped and armed."

The conversation resulted in a serious consultation with Veo as to the proposed trip abroad.

"We have three thousand dollars left, Veo, and that would buy a pleasant little home in Iowa where we could reside—"

"Yes; but Elbert, you are too ambitious to be satisfied there."

"Well, there's my little wife—"

"Elbert, your little wife is you.   Your ambitions are my ambitions, and if you need to travel in Europe, why, we'll go."

"It is placing all our fortune on the hope of my achievements when we return."

"Never mind that, Elbert.   We'll invest that five thousand dollars in prospective achievements."

"My inspiration," he said, as he kissed her.

CHAPTER XIX.

"How much a dunce that has been sent to roam
Excels a dunce that has been kept at home."
—Cowper.

"Art is long, life is short; judgment difficult, opportunity
transient."
—Goethe.

"We are on a voyage to discover the world," wrote Veo to Agnes, "and Elbert is reversing the notions of Christopher Columbus. We are going east to discover a new route to India."

They had arrived in Germany the day previous, and Elbert at once began active preparations for his special study of the working classes in relation to the tariff question. He found it slow and awkward work, not being able to speak the language. He was regarded with more or less suspicion as a stranger, and finding many of the larger manufacturing establishments in Germany absolutely closed to strangers, even with letters of introduction, he was becoming disheartened.

"Never mind, dear, the note books will look better when we get home," said Veo. "Now let us enjoy our trip just as if we were millionaires and tourists."

They made a trip up the Rhine, and the old castles on either side seemed to bring a comprehension of the early history of Germany that no books could give. At Drachenfels the whole story of the castles of the

Rhine was recalled in a flood of sunlight, as they gazed
on the beautiful valley beneath, and the winding Rhine
fringed with historic mountains, crested with purple
forests and terraced with vineyards, and capped by
crumbling castle towers. Elbert enjoyed it all, and
yet felt a sense of guilt as if neglecting the specific
object of his visit.

They decided later to leave the well-worn path of
tourists and drifted to Weimar, the home of the poets
Goethe and Schiller, and a virtual Mecca in German
literature and music. They arrived on Sunday morning, when all nature was under the spell of the impressive quiet of the day. Were these the same sights that
inspired Goethe? Were these the same fields he had
gazed upon? This old gabled house, the deep ravine
and viaduct, the old pump—were these familiar to
Goethe, Schiller and Mendelssohn? They felt something inspirational as they passed Schiller's home,
that tall brick house with shutters close to the street.
Then around the corner the long low house where
Goethe had lived so many years. At the right of the
door as they entered was the low, broad, flat stairway of well-worn oaken steps. The view then pre-
sented of the long hall, with the statue of Juno; near
by the harpsichord on which Mendelssohn played,
seemed like a peep into the tomb of the past. Veo
sat down to the instrument and struck those massive
chords in the March of the Priests from Athalia, and
it seemed like a mysterious voice from the dead.
Everywhere in glass cases were the famous Goethe collection of medallions and the trophies bestowed upon

Germany's greatest poet. Then the library, the old pine desks, the chair and table where the poet sat and dictated in his declining days, even the elbow cushion upon which he rested his arm when bowing his head in thought, still remained. Just off the library was a small room with a wainscoting of green cloth, containing a couch covered with a faded pink spread. In the corner was the table upon which the cup and saucer and some medicine bottles still remained as when he died. At the foot of the bed the old casement window was swung open, and the branches of the tree just outside had grown closer as if to shelter the nook where Goethe had closed his eyes in eternal slumber as his soul passed away to greet his own Marguerite.

"Oh, Elbert," whispered Veo, "such scenes as these are inspiring. We never can forget this day."

They stood arm in arm for some moments, feeling the kindly spirit of the poet upon them.

Every day was crowded to its fullest capacity with sight-seeing. Baedeker was thrown aside for real impressions, and they drifted on and on without specific purpose.

At one of the hotels in Frankfort they met Mrs. W. Dannocks Daniels, widow of a United States army officer, whom Elbert had met at Bart's home and at Springfield. It was of course a surprise to see her, but in a foreign land a very slight previous acquaintanceship is accepted as friendship of long years' standing. She was a bright talker and an old traveler, and while they had met many other Americans and made other friends during their travels, Mrs. Daniels was

an especially attractive acquaintance. She was well
versed in art and literature, and she and Elbert enjoyed
many Platonic discussions during the days the three
were sight-seeing together. Even Veo fell quite in
love with her.

While in Paris Elbert acquired his first real taste for
art. Mrs. Daniels was with them to discuss together
the paintings of the masters, but Veo was more interested in studying the students on the scaffolds and
in dark corners at the Louvre, who were trying to
imbibe the spirit of the great painters. Rubens with
his plump women and idyllic hazel eyes, and rich lurid
coloring, never fails to attract the admiration of the
novice. Rembrandt's sober backgrounds brought
back to Veo a happy day at The Hague, where she
had idealized the little painting of his mother.

The sights of Paris were one series of wonderment
and delight. The Pantheon, Madeline, Arc de Tri-
omphe, Place de la Concorde, the Juli Column, all
rich with historical associations, from these Elbert
got that swift and realistic comprehension of history
so different from that of the class-room. In France
he felt in sympathetic touch with the American idea,
and as he stood by Rousseau's statue near the Pantheon he realized that the great philosopher had been
one of the leading spirits in the era of agitation which
resulted in American independence. But Elbert made
little or no progress in the study of the tariff question.
At Versailles and Luxembourg, Elbert and Mrs. Daniels reveled in Platonic discussions, and their tastes
quite harmonized

"Your predilection is literary rather than political, Mr. Ainsworth," said Mrs. Daniels one day.

"That may be true, but my absorbing ambition is political, and our aspirations rather than our tastes govern us."

"Perhaps; but how much more one achieves in following what one loves."

"But our ability often does not harmonize with our aspirations."

"Then why oppose the inevitable?" she insisted. "If you knew what I do of Washington and of Washington political life, political ambition would not lure you further."

This conversation Elbert considered a temptation to divert him from his real ambition, and then he pinched himself to bring to mind those tariff statistics.

At Brussels they found a petite Paris. The Palais de Justice may be grander in architecture than the capitol at Washington, and yet how insignificant the comparison as to what each represents. The presence of soldiers at every entrance and avenue to public buildings throughout Europe was a decided contrast to the wide open gates at the white house and public grounds in Washington.

It was in Brussels that Veo was taken ill.

"Too bad; the first day I've missed. But, Elbert, you and Mrs. Daniels must go."

"No; I'll stay here, Veo, and—"

"But I'm not that ill. Now, that's a good boy; go along."

Elbert and Mrs. Daniels visited the sights of Brus-

sels together and continued their discussions. At the
Wertz museum they disagreed again in a good-natured
way.

"There is something impressively grand in this
place," she said, enthusiastically.

"It reminds me more of a chamber of horrors! Of
all the ghastly sights on earth—buried alive—mother
burning her child—Napoleon in hell—"

"But we must know the realities of life; these paintings have a mission."

"The particular mission must be to induce suicide.
Even the Homeric Patroculus and all of his heroic
paintings have that insane and desperate look. It
makes it appear almost a blasphemy where they pur-
port to portray the face of Christ."

"But how masterly the strokes! And coloring almost
equal to Rubens!" she urged.

"Yes; they show vigorous muscular power at least."

"But the little sketches of each painting indicate
painstaking work at least. That painting of himself,
however, shows the man—"

"An egotistic cynic, and cynics are useless in the
world."

As they were leaving the vine-covered building, a
man coming from the gallery opposite approached
them.

"My dear Mrs. Daniels, how delighted I am to see
you," said the stranger.

It was all said in a breath, and the familiarity net-
tled Elbert. The stranger was finally introduced as
Captain Pardemore, U. S. A., and he asked to call

and see Mrs. Daniels that evening, as he left them. Mrs. Daniels was quick to read human nature, and she watched Elbert's face intently on the meeting with Captain Pardemore.

"A charming fellow—he wants me to join him," she said, sweetly.

"Mrs. Daniels, do you ever have sincere attachments for friends?" asked Elbert, solemnly.

"Yes, I love my friends. Friendship is one of the noblest ties that bind two individuals."

"But there are more sacred ties," remonstrated Elbert.

"Yes; but love and true affinity come first. My impulse is to find happiness only in love irrespective of conventional decrees. Why restrict ourselves to Puritanic custom? Too often people are legally bound to uncongenial spirits, and I choose to declare my independence as an individual."

"You don't mean that you would travel alone with this man?"

"No, I am not an adventuress; he is not the man. But with one I loved I would dare the world's scorn, and be—happy."

She was beautiful in her earnestness and seemed to believe what she said. Their eyes met. It was an instant of temptation, but a face flashed upon Elbert. Two innocent eyes that reflected a soul came before him. It was evident to Elbert that he was in danger and that the spell must be broken, as Mrs. Daniels was truly a fascinating woman. In fighting temptation he felt that the opportunity must first be banished.

CHAPTER XX.

"And I could not speak for wonder; but he spoke with a
murmur like the dying away of a beat upon a bell."
—John Ruskin.

Without even saying good-bye to Mrs. Daniels,
Elbert and Veo left Brussels. Veo was astonished,
but asked no further questions when Elbert told her
that he must not loiter in leisure. They went direct
to England, where Elbert really began his actual work
of investigation. In fact, he became a real workman,
donning workman's clothes and entering enthusiastically into his investigations. He discovered facts never
before disclosed to his mind, and the longer he investi-
gated the more thoroughly he became convinced that
protection was the right policy for the United States.
He found the condition of workingmen in many parts of
England deplorable. This was the competition American workingmen must meet with in open markets. English factories were then anxiously waiting for American
tariff legislation to enable them to place their goods
on the American market. Elbert had many heated
discussions with English friends, all of whom believed
their interests were those of the United States. His
natural sympathies were with the working classes, and
he felt a selfish interest in the laboring men of his
own country. The experiences of those few months
were an education in political economy such as years

in the study of the theories of Adam Smith and John Stuart Mill could not furnish. Actual experience and facts gained by induction forged an opposite conclusion to that of the free trade deductive and seductive theories.

In his recent reading on the subject, Elbert had found in John Ruskin a partial apostle of his absorbing idea of protection. After a visit to the Turner room in the National Gallery in London, Elbert felt that he must see John Ruskin while the sage of Brantwood yet lived, and feel the inspiration of that great thinker's presence. In another week they were enjoying all the beauties of the lake district, visiting Ambleside, Ryddle, Grassmere and Dentwater. The coaching tour to Coniston, up the famous Yewdale valley immortalized by Wordsworth, Southey and Coleridge, gave Elbert a subtle comprehension of these English poets not achieved by students of English literature in the atmosphere of a class-room.

At Coniston Elbert found the villagers shaking their heads in a mysterious way when he talked of seeing John Ruskin. But few neighbors were familiar with his books, and yet all seemed to love him. Brantwood, the home of the sage, was across the lake, directly opposite the village. Elbert ascertained that the aged philosopher took a walk from Brantwood to a little point of land farther up the lake, where he would sit for hours and watch the waves of Coniston wash upon the pebbly beach. Brantwood is a stone slate house covered with white stucco and festooned with Virginia creeper. It looked an ideal philosopher's re-

treat among the bleak and wrinkled peaks, fringed at
the base with forest and festooned with heather. Elbert
rowed across the black waters of the lake to a point
just above where the sailboats were moored opposite
the home. Clambering up through the brush to the
road he passed little bits of pasture, orchards, flower
and vegetable gardens, all nestling at the foot of the
rugged hills. The stone hut of a farmer in a sterile
field farther up the hill indicated that at least one
neighbor was within hailing distance of the lonely
sage of Brantwood. Elbert approached the house with
awe through a tunnel of foliage. He pulled the bell,
but there was no response.

"I came to see John Ruskin, and they cannot kill
me for it," he thought, as he stood trembling before the
door.

He rang again, and a maid in a white cap came to
the door. Elbert asked to see Mr. Severns, the artist
who is the husband of Mrs. Ruskin's niece.

"He is very busy," was the answer.

"Tell him a gentleman from America wishes to see
him."

When she had retired Elbert stood in the little hall,
with its red ingrain carpet, hungrily drinking in all
of the details. On the wall directly in front hung a
charcoal sketch by Burne-Jones. A door led from the
hall on either side, and the sound of a voice in the
stillness thrilled the visitor. Could that be Ruskin's
voice?

Mr. Severns came down soon after, and Elbert in
a confused way confessed his mission.

"It is not a pleasant intrusion, and you Americans are so impertinent," said Mr. Severns, sharply.

Elbert made another plea, more in his looks than by words, and he was shown into Ruskin's study at the right of the hall. His first glance rested upon a little straight-backed chair, upholstered in green. This was the favorite seat of the sage. On the table and in the French window were flowers in slender glass vases. Above the mantel was his famous collection of Greek relics. On the walls hung various sketches in charcoal indicating Ruskin's favorite study of ancient architecture. The little clock on the wall kept ticking away those precious minutes which were to leave impressions for a lifetime on Elbert. Underneath the bookcases surrounding the room was Ruskin's famous geological collection, suggesting a similarity in taste with that of the poet at Weimar. There seemed to be an innate passion in these two great minds to collect the actual expressions of Nature. The graceful drapery of Virginia creeper over the casement at Brantwood brought to mind the old tree at Weimar.

And yet, John Ruskin was not there.

Elbert passed out of the house absorbed in his hero worship. Passing through the arched driveway which penetrated the south wing of the house, he suddenly came upon a sight which thrilled him. A tall, yet stooped form, one shoulder much higher than the other, with his long gray beard buttoned inside his coat, shaggy and fierce-looking eyebrows under which sparkled kindly gray eyes; on his head a white slouch hat, his hands behind him grasping a walking stick, moving along slowly followed by his valet at a respectful distance. This was John Ruskin.

Elbert was so occupied with his thoughts that he could not speak. He followed the aged seer into the house, but not a word was spoken. Ruskin took his seat in the little green chair at the window. Elbert stood near by as if hypnotized. Directly opposite the window on the banks of the lake was an old tree, the top branches of which had been wrenched off by a storm. A mass of ivy hung about the tall protruding trunk, as if to hide the ravages of the tempest, and the wide-spreading lower branches seemed outstretched in benediction as the sunlight played on the black waters of Coniston. How like the sage of Brantwood! His life broken and saddened by storm and tempest, and yet clinging about it were the brightest and sweetest memories, his words resting like a benediction upon the hopes of the young and ambitious. Elbert left the house feeling as if his living idol had remained in the tomb, drifting from the terrestrial to the celestial. Call it foolish sentiment, but those few hours at Brantwood emphasized Elbert's ideal of pure manhood. It was one of those events which determine destiny. The spark of an uncompromising ambition had been ignited.

For several hours that evening Elbert was busy relating to Veo the veriest trifle connected with that visit to Brantwood, which together they considered the crowning achievement of their tour. "Unto this Last" was now read with new zest and understanding, and

"Sesame and Lilies" had created a new comprehension of the problems of life.

"Veo, if the world demands a sad and pathetic career for all of its great men, I believe I will stop right here," said Elbert.

"Elbert, the great men do not have all the sorrow. We all bear our burdens, and theirs seem great simply because they are brought into greater prominence."

"But many writers appear to linger on the great griefs of genius as its inspiration."

"Well, Elbert, just have faith; that does away with fears and tears. And now I'm trying so hard to read and admire Ruskin—"

"My little wife must not work too hard."

"Well, Elbert, if I can only make you happy, I don't care whether I can understand Ruskin or not."

"You do make me happy, little one; but must I keep on saying it every day?"

"Every hour, Elbert; a woman's heart is always hungry for a kind word from the man she loves."

He drew her closer to him. The memory of Mrs. Daniels and her philosophy had vanished.

CHAPTER XXI.

"A mother's pride, a father's joy."
—"Rokeby," Sir Walter Scott.

Financial problems have an uncomfortable way of presenting themselves to disturb poetic fancy. Money is one of the essentials of modern life, and Elbert discovered that the remnant of his financial reserve had nearly vanished. As if to make the best of it he remarked:

"Well, Veo, I am longing to return to America, anyhow, where everyone does not walk on tiptoe."

"So am I, Elbert. Those continental breakfasts of coffee, rolls and honey are civilized starvation."

"We've plenty of note books if we are rather short on tariff facts," said Elbert.

The stay in England somewhat modified Elbert's radical ideas. He realized that America with all its boasting was only a part of the universe after all; that even hated corporations are in a way a special benefit to public weal; even royalty was not altogether obnoxious. In fact, without having his loyalty to American institutions shaken, his observation had broadened his ideas beyond the mere localized egotism of his own country. Even Veo sadly confessed.

"Yes, we do talk through our noses, and say 'I guess' and 'ain't,' and measure everything by bigness, but

that includes big hearts in America, while in England
it is big I's and big heads. I don't like English con-
ceit, even if it is reticent and well-bred. I am longing
for the free air of the old farm and Poplarville, Elbert,"
said Veo, enthusiastically.

"We'll soon be there, pet."

A few weeks later they were at the old home in Poplarville, but it did not seem home to Veo. Elbert was
looked upon as a failure as a city attorney, and a
foolish young chap who had spent everything he had
in travel and had now returned to live upon the farm,
waiting for the demise of Veo's father. At least this
appeared to be the suppressed impression of the neighbors. Elbert soon realized the suspicions, and his
proud spirit was aroused, and he chafed under what
he felt to be a cloud; but he continued his work of
collating notes and preparing for the fall campaign.
The village gossips insisted that he was lazy and shift-
less, and was living upon his wife's father as a pensioner. It all stung him, but he toiled on in patience.

The rivalry in small villages of church societies is
about the most marked feature of their social life. The
missionary teas and mite societies are held for "our
church."

In every community there must be a division of
some kind, and as in Poplarville they were all practi-
cally of one political belief, three hundred and twelve
votes year after year in Buzzard township. The church
societies had to take up the cudgel to keep up the
life of the place. One church assumes a patrician air
as the leader in social life and the others dispute it.

The question comes up at every turn in public affairs,
"Is he a Presbyterian, is he a Methodist, or is he a
Catholic?" Positions on school boards, road supervis-
ors, village trustees, all came under a semi-sectarian
inspection. And yet after all it was a pure and wholesome life. Open-hearted and generous, such a thing
as a case of real poverty was scarcely known in the
township. The little rivalries were for a good purpose
and the public officers imbued with the right spirit.
Churches and schoolhouses flourished as the flowers
of perfected civilization.

The village life of his own birthplace was an interesting study to Elbert. His travel had enabled him
to observe with the right perspective. The individual-
ity of American villagers was in sharp contrast to the
passive and ambitionless existence of similar classes
in Europe.

But Elbert waited an event.

It was the night of suspense which all young fathers
remember when the first baby was born. Elbert had
rushed for Dr. Buzzer, who came down the lane talking and puffing vigorously.

"You young fellows get fearfully excited, by ginger,"
he said. "Now you just let me watch this affair and
I'll see that Veo comes out all right. Time you've
had nine or ten you'll not be so nervous, young man."

The young mother was cared for by Mrs. Ainsworth,
with a tenderness almost equal to that of her own angel
mother. "God save little Veo," was the continuous
prayer of Elbert during those terrible hours of suspense.

The little red-faced infant was placed in his arms. What a thrill it gave him. "My child! Veo's baby!" Later he walked into the darkened room.

"Our own baby. Are you happy, Elbert?" whispered Veo.

"My precious wife; my queen!"

The little babe began to cry.

"Our dear little baby," whispered Veo, and her face was wreathed in a radiant, angelic expression which only young motherhood can give—an inspiration for a Raphael's Madonna.

A father! Elbert could scarcely realize it. All other ambitions now fade—for wife and baby come first. "Oh, God, I thank Thee for Thy goodness," he prayed inwardly, and felt the presence of Deity impelling that secret prayer which many men express in a crisis, although they may be loth to acknowledge it later.

CHAPTER XXII.

"Whose armor is his honest thought,
And simple truth his utmost skill."
                                    --Sir Henry Wolton.

The realization that he was now a "family man" awoke Elbert to the fact that he must make some arrangements for an income. He decided to go direct to Washington, and be in touch with the political powers that "expect to be" before starting on his campaigning tour. It was the first time he had been parted from Veo since their wedding, but it must be done. The baby Veo was flourishing, and now he felt that the child would naturally take some of the affection Veo had showered upon him, for while a child unites man and wife in a holy parental tie, it also divides them.

When he arrived in Washington, he found there were scores of others like him awaiting the result of the election for "a plum." His record in Chicago confronted him, and he was looked upon by jealous rivals as a renegade, having changed his political beliefs to suit the shifting political winds. Matters began to look very discouraging, when Elbert was introduced to a member of the President's cabinet at the Willard. They were taking an evening smoke in the hotel office, when Elbert in the course of conversation told him of his situation.

"Bad thing, this depending on politics, young man. That's why I'm a horse doctor," said the secretary, stroking his long, gray beard, with a twinkle in his eye.

"And here I am, loaded and primed for the campaign, but no assurance even for expenses, let alone anything later."

"Well, now, just keep a stiff bit, young man, and we'll see what can be done. But the minute you can quit politics as a business, do it."

"If it were not for wife and baby—"

"Yes, yes, I understand," broke in the secretary; "we'll have to see what can be done. You come with me to New York next week and we'll see how the Central Committee commissary feels. You better go back home and work up. We all have to serve a political apprenticeship, you know."

This was the first ray of hope for Elbert, and he spent the intervening time preparing his speeches. But the events of that week shriveled his ideals of American statesmen. The "Division" in Washington tells the story. Congressmen, politicians and clerks openly and defiantly assailing all the tenets of pure manhood.

"Why, it is necessary to go through these experiences, Ainsworth, to be a well-rounded man of the world," said an acquaintance to Elbert one evening at the hotel.

"What, defile a home and deceive a trusting wife?"

"Oh, well, that is how you look at it. There are some who can get along and not go through the mill,

but they are few and their career is decidedly incom-
plete."

"I'll have to allow my career to stop right here,
because I consider that my manhood comes first."

"I'm surprised, Ainsworth, that a man who has traveled as much as you have should not have his eyes
opened. It's only a little relaxation, and prudes don't
always prosper in Washington. They are nondescripts."

"You have indeed opened my eyes, my friend. If
such immorality and lechery exists as you say, the
corruption of the Roman empire was nothing in comparison, but rest assured there is a final accounting
for all these things."

"Bother! This thing is the story of centuries. There
are few great men who have not had their mistresses."

"No man is great who has wilfully degraded himself, and I'm quite willing to take my chances with the
nondescripts," said Elbert excitedly.

The revelation was indeed astounding. Public men
whose names were on every lip and even household
words parading on Division at night like skulking
Satans.

The conference in New York was successful. It is
prominent political friends who help their successors
to places on the political chessboard, and when Elbert
was known as "the secretary's friend" that was enough.
The dates were arranged and he donned the political
armor for the campaign. A few speeches in the New
England states did not attract any especial attention, but in these he was only rehearsing his work.

Later on he appeared with men of national reputation, and his vigor, his eloquence, his thorough knowledge of the questions at issue, his living pictures of the actual condition of European workingmen under free trade soon made him felt as a power in the campaign field. He was called the "young whirlwind," and his caustic and sharp fighting qualities brought him to Indiana, Ohio and the other close states. The Central Committee no longer haggled over his expense account. In those few months he proved the man, possessed the theme, and improved the occasion which made him one of the foremost of the new orators in the campaign. The speeches were considered too melodramatic for permanent influence, but he always carried the throng with him in spite of the severe criticism of the opposition newspapers.

His speeches brought a letter from one of the friends who had urged his trip abroad.

"I am gratified to know you took my advice and are meeting with such unqualified success. You know your facts, you feel your theme, you speak from observation and experience. Is the lesson not better learned than from text-books.

Elbert's success quite naturally came very near turning his head, but in the exciting whirl of the campaign, two or three letters a week reached him from "Your own Veo and Baby," which managed to hold him quite level. He remembered after all who he was and what he had been a short time before.

"I want to speak at Poplarville, Iowa," he said to the chairman one day.

"That's a small town for you and time is pressing."

"Yes, but it's my old home and my wife and baby are there."

He had his way and his other important dates were canceled.

CHAPTER XXIII.

"If two lives join, there is oft a scar."
-"By the Fireside," Browning.

What a thrill passed over Elbert when he arrived at Poplarville a few evenings later. The Poplarville country brass band was there and started in full blast the moment he appeared. Cheers rent the air and the torch lights smoked vigorously. The lurid reflections cast in all directions gave the scene a weird aspect that suggested the meeting of the ancient Druids, or a caucus in the catacombs of Rome. Elbert took his place in the carriage beside Dr. Buzzer, who was chairman of the "Committee on Reception."

"We'll have a great old crowd for you to-night, my boy; always said so; but if you spring any more of those political horse chestnut jokes in this neighborhood I'll not promise to protect you. You must give it to 'em straight and pop it to 'em on the prohibition question, for that's the ticklish end of the mule just now."

Elbert was taken to his mother's home. Just a minute to kiss wife and baby and partake of a bit of supper, and the Committee arrived to escort him to the corners in a blaze of triumph. Hundreds of people had gathered there, the farmers having driven in for

miles around, and the torches gave the corners a holi-
day glare. The brass band scarcely ceased playing. It
was an inspiring scene, and when Elbert arrived there
was a wild shout. He spoke as he had never spoken before, feeling that he knew each individual hearer and
his simple story arose to dangerous heights of eloquence. The speech did not appear to awaken the
enthusiasm anticipated. In fact the meeting that
had started in so gloriously had rather chilled at its
close.

"Oh, we expected too much, perhaps. It's only
Elbert Ainsworth."

"The same old speech he's been giving months. I've
read it a dozen times in the papers."

These were some of the expressions of the dispers-
ing throng. On the other hand, he had a number of
friends who after the address gathered about to congratulate and shake hands with him. He was about
to start home with Dr. Buzzer when a woman came
toward him.

"You here?" said Elbert.

"Yes, Elbert; I'm here where I started years ago
to begin life over, and have accepted the school for a
year."

It was Mrs. Waldie, his school teacher.

"Why, what is the cause of this?" he inquired.

"It is a long story, Elbert, and I'll not stop now to
relate it. You did us proud, my boy, to-night, and
you'll succeed."

"Come and stay with us. Have you seen Veo?"

"I will see you all to-morrow," she said quietly, as she left him.

*   *   *   *   *   *   *   *

After Bart's quarrel with Elbert, and the revelation of Paulina to Agnes of Bart's past life, husband and wife drifted farther apart. Agnes made frequent and long visits to Poplarville, and the gypsy seemed to shadow her until the villagers began talking. It was during the absence of Elbert and Veo abroad, that Jasper Juniper, as justice of the peace, became interested. He got an inkling of Paulina's story and went to see Bart in Chicago.

He had known Bart's parents in Indiana before removing to Poplarville and felt interested. Bart was surprised to see him.

"I took the first train yesterday from Poplarville. Plutarch says: 'When you've business with a man go and see him, don't write.' So here I am. Bart, I must see you. Sit down there, man, and listen to me. I've known you since you were knee high to a grasshopper, but what I want to know is, is there any truth in what they say?"

"I don't know. What do they say?" answered Bart, languidly.

"Well, for years off and on some Bohemian or Hungarian, or gypsy woman—'pears to me more like a devil than a Christian—well, this woman has been living in Poplarville doing washing. She gave out that she had left a band of gypsies at Davenport or Dubuque or somewhere. Had renounced the tribe or something, and wanted to earn an honest living in our village. Of course everybody gave her work and she lived among us. Well, every three months or so, she would disappear. No one thought anything about it, knowing her gypsy habits. Then she'd come back, sometimes sad, sometimes gay. Well, this has been going on for two years and a half.

"One time I heard of her and 'Snakes' havin' a little spat, but I thought nothing of it. 'Snakes' complained at that time that Paulina—that's the woman's name— had taken a picture that her mother had given her, but we thought nothing of it. Abner Tomer was for having her arrested and brought before me on the charge of larceny. But I pooh-poohed, I didn't want no fee out of 'Snakes'' trouble. Now it appears why Abner wanted her arrested. Well, nothing happened with Paulina till a few days ago. Agnes had come down, you know—for—well—for a visit. She goes to Mrs. Ainsworth's. Don't find the children there, so she goes to Chatsworth's. I found out, unbeknown to any, that the devil of a Paulina comes to Chicago and saw your wife. Now what passed is not quite certain, but things began to be whispered around the village, ugly things against you being married before, and about 'Snakes.' Bart, my boy, I traced them all to this Paulina. I sent the deputy sheriff for her. I examined her, and now, Bart, I want to know if the mess of stuff she told me is true or not."

"Uncle Jasper, I think—"

"Answer me, my boy; I am your father's old friend. What relation have you with this woman? Does she speak the truth? Agnes may be to you the same as ever, but her heart is crushed. So here I am to know; does this she-fiend speak the truth?"

"Partly yes and partly no."

"Out with it, then; give me the facts."

"When I left dear old Mount Ariel I thought it would be a great thing to have money, swing precincts and all that sort of thing. The little money I made from my first contract I squandered with the boys. You know how it goes. Well, one night in a little hell on Clark Street a flower girl came in. Beneath the rags there was beauty, yes, refinement. The girl struck my fancy—God forgive me—I picked her up— Oh! I cannot, I cannot—" he broke down, with his head upon the table.

"And this Paulina?" asked Jasper.

"Is her mother. I never loved her. But she, she gave me all that a woman can give—her body, her soul, her all; and I, the miserable wretch that I was, thinking that the life of a sport, a ward bummer, a pot-house politician, was the road to fame and wealth, taunted by the boys with the sophistry of the saloon— every public man must have his mistress—I fell. Oh, Uncle Jasper, can you conceive for one moment the cancerous conscience that I have carried around with me these years?"

"And where is this woman?"

"In New York. I have since sent her a weekly allowance."

"Her mother says you were married to her daughter."

"Never."

"But she shows a marriage certificate."

"Another evidence of my weak folly. Her mother sold her to me for five hundred dollars. Finding I could not rob her of her virtue, she—she is a noble, pure, true woman—I am the guilty wretch—we pretended to be married. Uncle Jasper! Life is real, earnest, weak, passionate, devilish, tender, pathetic, true, and false. Have you any idea—you, living in the quiet, peaceful, pastoral simplicity of Poplarville—have you any idea how many times a day, in this great city of Chicago, in every city of the world, every day in the year, some man is deceiving some woman? Oh! for my mother! my mother!"

"Yes, she died soon after poor Wesley's death, and never knew this, Bart."

"One minute. I have nothing to say in defense, only this—that before marrying Agnes I determined to reform, sent Naomi to New York, paid Paulina two thousand dollars for all claims and the surrender of the false certificate. I have it here, meant to destroy it long ago. Gone! That she-devil has stolen it." He found the paper had been taken from his desk.

"Then you have seen her since you broke with her?"

"Yes; she has followed me up until my life has been a hell, a living hell."

"There's something more—"

"No; nothing more."

"Hints are thrown out about 'Snakes.' This Paulina says—"

"She would dare to say anything. But as God is

my living judge, Naomi is the only woman I have deceived."

"Abner was telling me something about a picture of yours, which this Paulina brought you after Elbert's wedding."

"How did you know that Paulina brought me any picture? Here is the picture," he said, pulling out the likeness from his desk. "It is one I sent to mother years ago. A birthday present. She wanted one. I supposed Paulina had stolen it to frighten more money out of me."

"Bart, I know you to be a man of generous, warm-hearted impulses. Everybody in Poplarville has felt your kindness and loves Agnes. Mary Jane, me, the doctor, everyone. These things pain us all. What can I tell them?"

"Tell them the truth. Tell them that only those who have been tempted in city life can judge. They will not be hard upon me."

"Perhaps not; only skinflints like Abner. You have tried to repair the wrong—in part—Agnes will forgive you. Tell her the truth yourself."

"I cannot—you tell her. I have tried to be a good husband to her. I love her truly, devotedly."

"I believe it. You should have told her yourself before you were married. Your passionate nature makes you strong friends, equally strong enemies. You cherish bitter feelings; sometimes beyond reason. There's Elbert, for instance."

"Why did he not stick to his friends? I stick to mine."

"Yes, I know; but his mind moves in a different channel. In Fowler on Common Sense, for instance—"

Agnes came in just then and greeted them both with a sad smile.

"Agnes, let Jasper tell you all—Paulina—"

"Not yet, Bart; I—"

This was the brief and unfortunate speech that aroused Bart's fury.

"Not yet? See, Jasper, that is the woman of it; they never forgive."

"But, Bart, listen," said Jasper.

"I will not listen. It is all over between us," he replied, fiercely.

"Agnes, you better go; I cannot stand this cool scorn," he continued, turning away with suppressed feeling.

"Bart, as you will; but I remember my duty as a wife—"

Bart had rushed out of the house without a good-bye.

There was a flood of tears, and Jasper tried to comfort the weeping wife as best he could.

"Mrs. Waldie, I don't know what to say. But come to Poplarville and teach again. It will all come out right sometime."

Married life was a puzzle to Jasper, and Agnes went to Poplarville.

CHAPTER XXIV.

"No man's pie is freed
From his ambitious finger."
—Shakespeare.

New stars in the political firmament are regarded with more or less suspicion by older politicians. It takes something more than a public "hit" to gain a foothold. The active manipulators have the machinery well in hand, and it requires a similar agency to gain a foothold.

When a young politician's power is well defined and his strength proven by a positive following, then thoughts are seriously entertained of admitting him as a possibility. Elbert discovered the process of slow growth. Following his success as a campaign orator, he thought a congressional nomination would only be the expression of the wish, but he found the ambitions of several wealthy men in the way. They looked for it as the reward of long years of party service and contributions to political campaign funds. He also observed that the most successful aspirants for political honors hailed from the country districts, where they were enabled to attach to themselves a loyal following, which the distracting jealousies of the city would not permit.

In carefully analyzing the situation he concluded to give up the practice of law in the city and begin a political apprenticeship in his own home district, realizing that his equipment for the profession of law was not sufficient to cope with the material turned out by the advanced law schools.

Elbert's new political wires were laid by having friends in Poplarville announce him as a delegate to the state convention. A systematic campaign was inaugurated on Bart Waldie's plan, carefully following up every possible advantage. The beginning was rather discouraging, as Elbert was regarded as an interloper by the men who usually "run things." But they had been in power so long that he conceived the idea of heading a movement against the old ring. He had the ready support of those disappointed in securing favors, and the periodical public spasm for a change was just then imminent. After a series of caucus contests he was successful in being named as a delegate to the state convention preceding the next general election.

The same reaction against the political powers that were in the saddle was apparent at the state convention. The cry of the opposition was to "give the young men a chance," and Elbert was not overlooked, and the constant recurrence of his name in print, even though the object of vituperative abuse, he viewed with complacent satisfaction. It is the old theory of sarsaparilla and pills, and too much abuse is better than fainthearted praise, he meditated.

At the state convention he was on the ground early, making acquaintances and forming all sorts of combinations. He assumed a positive strength, having first united the delegates from his district by making up a slate with four state officers upon it, so that if the first failed there would be three chances left. He became the particular champion of the farmer boys, and his familiarity with political and parliamentary tactics at once gave him prominence.

"We must ask for everything and keep up a bold front, or we will get nothing," was Elbert's admonition to his colleagues.

The contest was waging between two dividing factions in the state, headed by two of the prominent men. The weaker side at once sought a conference with Elbert, and he named the terms. The preliminary organization, the temporary chairman's address, and the naming of the committees was completed at the morning session. Elbert and his district delegation were purposely ignored by the opposing powers who controlled the organization. At the recess this fact was used to further solidify his own delegation, and to bring into his camp all of the disappointed elements. Elbert ate no luncheon during the recess and at 2:30 o'clock was ready for the contest. He felt there was a fighting chance, although there were four important offices to fill and five candidates conceded as entitled to nominations. One of these men was from Elbert's district, a prominent man, but not a politician, and he naturally gave Elbert charge of his interests. To be frank, Elbert conceived the idea of making a show of a terrific fight for his man, but inwardly he wanted him beaten, because if defeated he felt the district delegation would stand closer together in the future, and it

would effectually dispose of his only rival for the future
honors he might desire.

The first ballot was a struggle between the Titans.
Elbert and his delegation remained true to their promise, and the "powers that be" narrowly escaped defeat.
Then Elbert arose, and in a passionate plea for peace
and harmony moved the nomination of the defeated
candidate by acclamation to the next important office,
thus breaking the slate. It was a surprise and carried,
fairly stampeding the convention. This left only two
candidates to be chosen from the three aspirants. Elbert tried in the spirit of zealous friendship to force
his district candidate on the next ballot. This aroused
the suspicion of the friends of the candidate next on
the list with whom Elbert had made a combination,
and they began to seriously fear for their own welfare.
The election of the two Titans representing opposing
forces indicated that one of the remaining candidates
must be offered as a sacrifice, and all of the perfected
combinations of the morning were at once thrown
into confusion. Friends became foes, and Elbert's man
was defeated on that ballot. This left only one place
and two candidates, and the defeat of Elbert's protege
in forcing the ballot ahead of the agreed programme
had apparently doomed his district's nominee to defeat.
As the nomination of the last opponent was being
made, Elbert heard whispers among his own delegation that he had sold them out, and he saw at a glance
that his first plan of shelving his rival would be fatal
to his own interests; they had surmised his purpose.
He arose and paid a glowing tribute to the opposing

candidate. It created a sensation and he followed with an eloquent plea for fair play, insisting that all of the nominees who had been named thus far were from one side of a dividing line in the state and that his own half of the state was not represented. The opposing candidate, he continued, was too fair a man and too loyal to his party to deny the entire western part of the state at least a show of representation on the ticket. He closed with an eloquent tribute to his party, saying that its traditions and principles would never countenance injustice; that his portion of the state was a great bulwark of the party, deserving recognition. The effect was felt, and his opponents of only a few moments ago became his allies, and his allies became his opponents; the latter made abusive speeches as to Elbert and his candidate playing them false. He pulled the coat tails of his colleagues who were on their feet anxious to reply to the implied insult. "We submit ourselves as martyrs for the harmony of the party; we ask this favor not for ourselves but for the entire western half of the state," said Elbert in closing the debate.

The result of the ballot was awaited with great suspense, and Elbert felt that he had lost. There was a wild cheer as the last district was polled, as the delegation had divided its vote, and it elected Elbert's man by five majority. The adherents of the second candidate whom Elbert had nominated by acclamation came to his rescue, although in the ballot just preceding they were avowed opponents. The delegation

from Elbert's district cheered wildly and he was made
the hero of the hour.

"Young man, you are an honor to our district," said
the successful nominee, shaking his hand, "and anything I can ever do for you, simply call on me."

Elbert did not forget the promise, as his thoughts
centered upon a certain congressional nomination that
fall. But there were many things yet in the way.

The stirring events of that state convention gave
Elbert not only a political prominence throughout the
state, but made him a person of particular importance
in his own congressional district. Each one of the
delegates went home feeling a special interest in him,
and his congressional candidacy a few months later
brought him a large number of active supporters. Yet
it is doubtful if he would have been able to have over-
thrown the established and decreed order of succession
and re-election, had it not been for the death of the
incumbent, who sought re-election, and the unsettled
political situation at that time. The cry of the dema-
gogue was loud in the land and shrewd politicians began to tremble. The congressional nomination was
secured by Elbert after an arduous campaign, and he
could scarcely conceive that the ambitions of his youth
were realized. But he had not been elected, and this
was the time of political landslides.

CHAPTER XXV.

"Every day brings a ship,
  Every ship brings a word;
Well for those who have no fear,
  Looking seaward,
  Well assured
That the word the vessel brings
Is the word they wish to hear."
                    —Emerson.

The campaign was near an end, and Elbert had returned home to spend election day with Veo, who had remained at Poplarville with her father during Elbert's campaign tour. Silas Chatsworth was standing at the window, and called out to Dr. Buzzer who drove past the door:

"Hey, Buzzer, have you voted yet?"

"No, not yet. I'm on my way for the judge. He's rather feeble of late, so I thought I'd tote him down in my rig."

"Get out the full vote if you can. Send down Shandy for my bay mare. All the horses are up in the village. The poor child's been ailing lately."

"Noticed that for the last week. Silas, look out for her; she has heart trouble, and any sudden excitement is liable to—"

"Better stop on your way back and take another look at her."

"Yes, I will," said the doctor.

As Elbert entered the room the farmer continued: "Elbert, are you going up to the village this evening? It's only an hour before the polls close. Seems to me you would be anxious to know how the thing stands."

"Can't tell; perhaps so. Veo's not well and I hate to leave her with the baby."

"Well, there's Snakes—and me."

"You! I fancy, father, your days for handling babies are gone by."

"Humph! A grandfather's hand is the hand of experience. Better not reflect on your Uncle Jasper that way."

Abner Tomer in passing looked in at the door and said, excitedly:

"Just looked in to say, Elbert, that you'd better go to Dunham's, over the river, if you don't want to get left on that precinct. They're ten ahead of ye, so I'm told, and paying three dollars apiece for votes, more'n a week's wages, by gosh."

"Mr. Tomer," said Elbert, drawing himself up proudly, "if I am elected to Congress it will be with clean hands; I wish no taint of bribing to be attached to my career."

Mary Jane swept into the room as busy as ever and disturbed the conference. "Elbert, Veo wants you quick. Abner, run down—that's if you can run, and send Jasper here. Veo's taken sudden and wants to see him. Oh, Abner, just go in my back door, no, tell Jasper to—tell him to bring me two yards of red flannel, he'll find it in my top drawer, and Abner, Abner—"

"Well, what is it?" growled the deacon, leaving.

"Tell him to bring my thimble on the window sill in the sitting-room," shrieked Mary Jane.

"Darn women, anyhow," mumbled Abner, and shuffled off.

"Can't find a decent thimble anywhere," continued Mary Jane. "Mrs. Chatsworth, dear Lucy, left a thimble on that window when she died; but land o' Goshen, that was five years ago. 'Snakes,' come here.

"Snakes" came in slowly in response to the call.

"Veo's worse and I sha'n't go home to-night. 'Sides, I 'spect Elbert will be elected to Congress to-day. If he is, everybody will be up here sure as gunpowder. Now hustle, and have everything that'll hold water clean and ready."

"Can I live here always, Miss Toots?" said Snakes. "That's until I go to mother—she's dead, but she talks to me every night. Mr. Chatsworth says I keep the flowers in order and the buckets filled, and never touch his shaving soap, and keep quiet when he reads the paper, and I want to stay."

"Yes, Snakes, as long as you are a good girl you can stay," said Mary Jane, still busy with her sewing at the window.

Elder Whoops at that moment drove by and Mary Jane saluted him:

"Elder, stop a bit; don't go by. How is Sister Whoops? Well, I hope? And all the olive branches, young and old, from Melancthon down to Victoria?"

"Sister Toots, middlin', thank you, middlin'."

"Any news?"

"None; just voted for Elbert. If he is elected say a good word for me. Tell him to have me appointed chaplain in the navy yard. I can fill the yard, and Sister Toots, if there's a small piece of your renowned pumpkin pie in the larder and a hunk of head-cheese, I can stay the inner man till I get home. It's no trouble, I hope."

"Not in the least, Elder. Just wait a minute," said Mary Jane, putting down her work and going out. Elbert assisted Veo into the room, gently supporting her in his arms.

"Why, there's Elder Whoops," said Elbert, pushing the chair in which he had placed Veo towards the window. "Good evening, Elder; been to town? How's the election?" continued Elbert.

"Yes; just been and voted for you. Drove in on purpose. The talk is that you will go to Congress by two thousand majority," said the elder, with a flourish of his whip.

"That'll be perfectly lovely," said Veo, with a quiet smile.

"I hope so, and yet I don't. Political honors do not appear the same to me that they did three years ago. I have seen too much rottenness of political life," said Elbert.

"Ah, if all men were honest and true to principle," said the elder solemnly.

"There you touch the sore spot in the body politic. Honesty and adherence to principle. I tell you, Elder, I would sooner cut my right hand off than have Tom,

Dick and Harry pass me with a sneer, saying, 'Oh, he's like the rest; he's feathered his nest.' That would be a pretty legacy to leave my Veo. A political swindler, a common briber, a robber of the people!"

"That's the reason we have elected you," said Jasper, just coming in. "We want one who is honest to represent us. Elder, how is the vote?"

"Here, Elder, better tie up and come in," broke in Mary Jane, returning with the pie.

"Can't stop, sister; it's growing dark and five miles to go. Thank you. Your pies are—dear me—we never stop talking of that wedding supper you got up for Veo," said the elder, taking large bites out of the pie.

"Why, that's nearly four years ago, Elder," said Veo.

"So long?" said the Elder, with his mouth full.

"We have decided to make this our home," said Veo.

"Where you'll live and end your days, I hope," said Mary Jane.

"Yes, I'll end them here," replied Veo, sadly.

"Veo, child, I can't bear to see you talk like that," broke in Jasper; "Elbert will take you to Washington; I am sure a change of climate—"

"Home, sweet word," broke in Veo.

"Jasper Juniper, I've been trying for ten minutes to get a word in edgewise. Did you get me the flannel?" broke in Mary Jane.

"Couldn't find it, so I brought you a piece of cotton," Jasper replied, meekly.

"Cotton! I don't want cotton. Now—"

"Whoa! Whoa!" said the elder to his horse, which was anxious to go, seeing Shandy come down the road. "Shandy, if you are determined to ride a bicycle don't frighten every four-legged critter on the high road. Well, good evening. Hope, Veo, you'll be around to-morrow. Put your feet in mustard water, and give her a hot lemonade, Mary Jane. Get up there.

"Now I can read my title clear,

'To mansions in the skies',"

sang the jolly elder as he drove off.

"Land o' Goshen! Nothing ready to give the boys, just a taste of acid with the water when they come to-night. I've got five pans of gingerbread baking and Snakes is cutting the ham. Now, fly, Shandy, and get some lemons," ordered Mary Jane.

"Take the bay mare, Shandy," said Farmer Chatsworth.

"Not much; I've got something that will fly by any gray or bay mare," said Shandy, as he mounted his wheel.

"Buzzer said he'd stop in a minute with the news," said Jasper, preparing to go, "but I can't wait for him. Mrs. Speigles wants her shoes to-night, and I've not finished that last volume of Plutarch's Lives. Then the boys want me to lead the procession to-night. Anything more you want, Mary Jane?"

"Come back surely, Uncle Jasper," called out Veo. "I've got something particular to say to you. I'm not strong and it is about 'Snakes'."

"Don't worry, Veo; I'll be back," called out the good-natured cobbler.

"Elbert, your ship is nearing port. I can almost see its sails near at hand. Will it bring the word you wish to hear. Alas! what tidings will it bring?" said Veo.

"My own little captain is nervous. My election is assured and good tidings are at hand."

But Elbert never forgot those words.

"What are you doing, Elbert?" continued Veo, as Elbert sat down to write at the table.

"I suppose the boys will call on me for a reply to-night if I'm elected. Must have something ready, you know."

"Let me sit here while you write," said Veo, sitting on the same chair behind him. "Just go on with your work; I won't disturb you."

"I never want you a moment from me, my precious wife; you are my inspiration, my pride," said Elbert, kissing her; "now, let me think: 'Fellow-citizens and neighbors'," read Elbert as he wrote, " 'I thank you for your good wishes; one of my first efforts in Congress will be—' "

"You can think while I sew, can't you?" broke in Veo.

"Yes, yes; now let me see, where was I? Oh, yes; —'efforts in Congress will be—will be to so adjust the agricultural and labor interests—'," continued Elbert, writing.

"I won't talk, Elbert, but when do you suppose Agnes is coming?"

" 'That the wage workers'," said Elbert, as he kept

on writing a moment without speaking. "What did you say?"

"Agnes; when will she come?"

"'Unquestionably the tariff interests'," said Elbert, going on with his writing. "Oh, Agnes; I suppose she will be down to supper—glad she is coming; want to see her about Bart," he said, writing all the time he was talking. "'Then the duty on steel rails—'"

"Oh, Elbert, that pen scratches so. It makes me nervous. Let me get you another. It acts as if it were vexed."

"This is all right; '—here in my old home where I was raised from a baby—'"

"Oh, Elbert, didn't you know the baby had a tooth?"

"Has it? Where from a tooth"—he scratched—"'from a baby—where the wool is raised on our own farms—where—the farmer—the baby, the home—'" He got up and threw the pen down in disgust as Veo arose from her chair.

"Baby's crying, Elbert; you won't mind it if I go and lie down a little while; I'm so tired—but I ought to help you."

"No, darling wife," he said, stooping and kissing her.

"It's getting pretty dark, hold me closer, Elbert. Will you be very, very sorry if I should die sometime?" she said, giving him that old, soulful glance.

"Don't talk that way, my little darling, don't."

"I can't help it, Elbert. I want, oh! so much, to see the old tree. Let's go there to-morrow with baby."

"Yes, certainly."

"Elbert, I can't live long; but, oh, I can't leave you and the baby."

"For God's sake, don't talk so, Veo. We are going to Washington, and the change——"

"Never for me, dear husband. Promise me that you will bury me under the old tree, our trysting place, near Jasper's shop and Mary Jane's home."

"Veo, I can't stand it. Buzzer says you are going to get well; to be better to-morrow. Of course, you will. You are only tired from moving."

"I'm so tired. Hold my hand, Elbert. Why, Elbert, you are weeping," said Veo, awakening suddenly; "I am so sorry. Don't, don't cry."

"No, pet, go to sleep," said Elbert, and he laid her down gently on the lounge.

"Here they come, the whole township; they can't keep up with the wheel," said Shandy rushing into the room as distant shouts were heard down the road, growing nearer and nearer.

"Elbert, they are coming," shouted Farmer Chatsworth.

"Hush. Veo is trying to sleep."

The shouts continued, with "Hurrah!" "Hurrah!" "Elbert is elected." "What's the matter with Poplarville?" "Three cheers for Veo!" and a mammoth bonfire was lighted just outside as the crowds gathered around the windows and veranda, the small boys perched in the trees and upon the long hitching posts in front.

In response to the general cry for a speech, Elbert

appeared at the window and begun: "Fellow-citizens! I thank you for your cordial demonstrations; for your confidence, for your interests in pure politics, for your——"

"Elbert, come here, quick; look at Veo," called Mary Jane.

When Elbèrt began speaking, Veo had raised herself on the lounge, and Elbert rushed to her, taking her in his arms. "Veo, look up, speak to me. Doctor, do something." The doctor felt her pulse, and shook his head. "What is life without my wife? My God, doctor, don't say she's dead," he moaned.

Dr. Buzzer went to the door and put up his hand; the shouts ceased in an instant, and even the flickering shadows of the bonfires began to fade away. Veo's parched lips had scarcely moved, but it was a good-bye. Elbert kissed her and laid her down, and left the weeping friends with his dead. Not a tear would flow. He was dazed. The huzzahs of the multitude a moment ago seemed like hollow mockery. Why should he have to lose her? Memories of their happy married life came rushing through his mind. Had he always been kind to her? Was his ambitious struggle worth anything without Veo?

A noise from the cradle started him. "Poor little motherless babe," he cried, and then the torrent of tears broke forth.

"Veo! Veo! My wife! My love! Speak again! My God, the light of my life has gone out!" and he sobbed over the cradle, mingling his cries with those of the motherless babe.

Elbert's ship had arrived. Death was at the helm, and Ambition, with a mocking smile, brought him the word he had longed to hear.

CHAPTER XXVI.

"Get thee behind me, Satan."—Holy Writ.

"If a due participation of office is a matter of right, how are vacancies to be obtained? Those by deaths are few, by resignation none."

—Thomas Jefferson.

Veo was buried under the fallen tree, as she had requested. It was a shock to the general notions of the community to have an interment anywhere but in the burial ground, but with Veo it seemed different. It was a sad funeral and nearly all the guests who were at the wedding were present.

To Elbert life now seemed blank and purposeless, but once again hearing his babe's plaintive cry he realized his duty. He left soon after for Washington to take his seat in Congress, and yet how empty the honor! In the first breath of political success he was as one dead, but in his grief he found an affection he had almost forgotten. When alone at night he would sit for hours and look at Veo's picture, then the baby's face smiled upon him. He felt the need of solace and comfort, but plunged into his work to forget his sorrow. Just before the new administration was to be inaugurated, Bart Waldie had been given his coveted appointment in Chicago. His "friends" said, "Give it to him. The other fellows will soon drop the axe on him, and that is the best way to pay our debts and dispose of him." A cold-blooded purpose, but immensely practical and popular in modern political ethics.

When the new administration had assumed control of affairs, Elbert made a special effort to prevent Bart from being removed, and his old political friends were shocked.

"Don't you know that he is one of the most perniciously active partisans on the list?" argued one to Elbert.

"That may be, but if he does his duty and makes a good officer, let him stay," replied Elbert.

"Yes, but if that rule is adopted what is there going to be left for us?" persistently argued one of his companions.

"That is all right, Tim, but I'll tell you why I'm so interested," and he told him of his past relations with Bart.

"Now, if it requires my share of appointments I'm going to give it up to keep Bart there," said Elbert decisively.

The decision of Elbert raised a furore among the multitude of office-seekers who had already swooped down upon Washington. He was charged with trying to create an office brokerage establishment, and being only a half-hearted convert to the new party—a spy whose mission was to keep in old appointees as far as possible. But he was firm and finally succeeded in obtaining a promise that Bart should serve out his term.

Bart could never quite bring himself to acknowledge

the favor from Elbert. It was not long after that, Agnes was called to Chicago by Bart's serious illness. She left at once with Mary Jane and nursed him back to health. But he still refused to acknowledge Elbert's kindness and Agnes wrote to Elbert to come at once, hoping to effect a reconciliation.

"Agnes, you know Elbert saved me my appointment? Well, if it were not for you I would throw it back in his teeth at once. I want nothing except from my friends."

Elbert and Jasper arrived at the house a few days later and found Agnes and Bart alone.

"How are you, Bart?" said Elbert, as he entered, extending his hand.

Bart was astonished at first, and then his eyes seemed to flash fire.

"I don't know you, sir. Oh, I remember. You are that goody-goody representative who was elected last fall; expect to reform things, don't you? Make men turn against their friends? Set up 'principle' and all that sort of thing? Introduce the millennium into Washington? Change human nature? Change human feelings?"

"That will do, Bart," responded Elbert calmly. "We haven't met for two years—it may be some time before we meet again—"

"Why did you force yourself here?" broke in Bart sharply.

"To hand you this letter from Washington, assuring me that as you are a faithful officer, though on the opposite side in politics, you will not be disturbed."

"At your request?" sneered Bart.

"At my request."

"Never—nothing from you, sir. Nothing from one who sold me out. I can never forget your perfidy—you're a traitor and·

"Bart!" cried Agnes and Mary Jane in chorus.

"Now, if you women would keep yourselves entirely out of my affairs, it would be better for all concerned."

"Bart, remember. You are older than Elbert," pleaded Jasper. "He has done you a good turn; take his hand—"

"Jasper, I appreciate your good intentions. Don't interfere. I may be needy, but nothing can ever bridge over the chasm between us. Keep the marshalship because he asked it? I think not," and Bart started to go.

"You should be grateful for his kindness to you, Bart, for our sakes."

"Agnes!" broke in Bart.

"I'm proud of him as my old pupil," she continued. "He has no resentment towards you; on the contrary that letter shows it. We should both be thankful."

"Stop!" he thundered, starting to go.

"No; as your wife I shall say what I please. I have before me daily, hourly, the direful, dismal effects of a political career. Thank heaven, just such a one as Elbert wishes to avoid. You will know what I mean."

"Would you nurse a viper?" hissed Bart.

"Bart, you are beside yourself," said Agnes, calmly. "We will not pursue the subject further. I have come home because you needed me. You are not the man you were three years ago. Dear Bart, let your nobler impulses rule. I am willing to forgive the past—to bury the dead. You are not so lost to a sense of honor, of your former noble self, as to refuse that letter, that kindness? Think! Night after night you have left me for heaven knows what—the dregs of politics. Days pass with scarcely a word from you. This and much more I am willing to forgive, because you need me. Elbert has done you no wrong."

"While I have breath I am master of this house," retorted Bart, pacing to and fro in the room like a madman.

"Bart, for my sake," pleaded Agnes, "for love of me take his hand. For Veo's sake; for Wesley's sake; for your mother's sake!"

This reference to his mother seemed to smite the rock. Bart's voice quivered, and Elbert went forward and Bart fell upon his shoulder and cried like a child.

"The day of Pentecost has come," shouted Mary Jane. "It is more blessed to give than to receive. Land o' Goshen, here I have left them eggs out to the front porch all this time. Merciful Providence, nobody took 'em," and she rushed out after them.

"Bart, you've showed your sense. Thrown the old boots away and begun on a new last," said Jasper, taking his hand.

"And by the Eternal, it shall last, Uncle," said Bart with tears still in his eyes.

"Elbert," said Jasper, "let's leave the young people together. Let's go out in the barn—Gee! I thought

I was to home—let's go out on the porch and swap lies. If I had a copy of Plutarch—"

"Agnes, I have much to say to you," said Bart to Agnes when they were alone, "Jasper has told me all."

"Not now, Bart, some other time. Do you not see I forgive you? Only be a man and give up this accursed anxiety, these disreputable associates. Be yourself, and I will always be your faithful, loving wife." For the first time in years he kissed her as a lover in response.

"I do not deserve to be so blessed, Agnes. For you I would do anything; I will resign, withdraw from active politics, attend to business. Make a home in the country, go to Europe; anything you like so long as you love me."

"Once more my noble husband!" said Agnes as they walked out arm in arm like real lovers. The storm was over; but they had scarcely left the room when Mrs. Daniels and Elbert came in. She was more dashing and more beautiful than ever.

"So glad to find you in town," she said to Elbert. "You got my last letter? And the wire congratulating you? Mrs. Waldie is still in Poplarville, I presume?"

"No, she is at home."

"Oh, then I should have asked for her. Now tell me your plans. Will you live at Willard's or will you take rooms? It is so much nicer to take rooms."

"You know my loss. Perhaps the hotel would be better."

"Poor, dear Veo; yes, I know. Oh, rooms are so

much more independent. Your friends may come and go when they please."

"I have no friends in Washington, except business friends."

"You naughty man; where do I come in?"

"You, of course; but I meant friends whom I could ask to my rooms."

"And why could you not ask me? Oh, we are quite unconventional in Washington. We do and think as we please; we do not mind public opinion. Now you must not forget your patronage. Many people will want to see you at your rooms. You silly boy, I must take you in hand. Senator Forthwith told me of that last foolish notion of yours. Do you know I had hard work to save you politically in this Waldie matter? What could possess you to demand his retention? You've weakened yourself."

"He is a good officer and my friend, and one to whom I owe much."

"You are guileless. Now you must do nothing without consulting me. You must ask for a reconsideration. Throw Waldie over and make yourself secure with your party workers. I will show you how."

"But, Mrs. Daniels—"

"No; no buts. It must be done. I came on to see about this matter. Of course Waldie expects to go out with the change of administration. All the judges say he never was strong in the marshalship. And there's Mrs. Waldie, with her quiet, refined ways, her dainty personality; how could she marry such an uneducated cad as he?"

"Mrs. Daniels, you must stop; I will not listen to such remarks. Mr. Waldie is not a cad; far from it. I have told you he is my friend. As a man he is the product of the self-reliant middle west, with all of the Chicago business push and political stickativity."

"There, don't be angry with me; but in politics, you know, we have no friends—outside of politics, yes."

"Friendship is one of the noblest ties that binds two individuals."

"But there are more sacred ties, I have heard you say before," she said archly and knowingly.

"Yes, I know the meaning of love. I look up constantly, expecting to see Veo. Her life was a sweet benison, a daily comfort. Her cheery voice is ever in my ears, ever present. I shall be very, very lonely."

"You need not be, Elbert. You and I are severely candid with each other on all subjects but one—the supreme passion. Ours is a true affinity. We both feel it. Let us put aside conventional and Puritanic decrees and live the life of real independence."

"Mrs. Daniels, I cannot listen to such sentiments— my Veo—"

"Where love rules, the world can be defied. My life in Washington has taught me the hypocrisy of the day. Why may not I speak my honest convictions? I am a lobbyist; I admit it; but even a lobbyist may love. And you have such a bright future; why half the world is miserable because of uncongenial surroundings. May not I help you?"

"Mrs. Daniels, my eyes are entirely open. You insult the memory of my wife. Please change the conversation. I will call Mrs. Waldie—I—if—"

"Be careful, Elbert, in your defiance. You know already what a woman's love is—do not crush mine. And a woman's scorn is hell let loose. Oh, Elbert, think; I may be lonely, too."

"Mrs. Daniels, any man would be blind who did not admire you. Admiration is the result of friendship. Love is another matter. I am grateful to you for your kindness. I appreciate your candor, but love and marriage between us—how can you suggest it—now, particularly?"

"We will drop the subject for the present. But, oh, Elbert; when a woman loves, she—we are disturbed; let us go into the parlor."

They left and Mrs. Daniels was deeply in earnest. The year was divisible by four.

CHAPTER XXVII.

"Till some chance thrill the loosened ruin launches
In unwarned havoc on roofs below."
—James Russell LowelL

Bart's determination to conclude his political career seemed to bring a cheerful air to his home, and among all the guests. Agnes was supremely joyful over her victory. It seemed now as if married happiness had only begun. As they were returning to the library they heard the maid arguing with some one.

"You cannot come in here; he is engaged."

At the door was Mother Madigan, saying, "Surely he'll not refuse to see one of his old pals," as she entered. "Tell him that I—

"Well, my good woman, who are you?" said Bart.

"Oh, you've forgotten Mother Madigan, Jimmy's mother? Many's the turn I've done him, mum," said the woman to Agnes. "Done it on the sly, when the wires were crossed or there was a bit of shindig to straighten out."

"That will do; what do you want?" asked Bart sharply.

"Jimmy's locked up—drunk last night. Jimmy, my son, ma'am, is the boss' best worker in our ward. Heaven bless the boy, and betune ye's and all harm, he's got the Boss more votes than all the sports a runnin'."

"Then it's money you want? You had better not wait, Agnes," said Bart, and Agnes left the room.

"As usual the law puts it, yer honor," continued Mrs. Madigan. "I am deprived of me daily support. There's not a happorth in sight, nor a crumb, and the devil knows how many days Jimmy'll get. I could not find you at the old place; so the officer sent me here."

Bart gave her some money and she stopped for breath: "May all the saints—"

"Now go; and never come here again," said Bart, turning to his desk.

As Mrs. Madigan started to the door she met Paulina coming in.

"Yes, yer honor, and may ye live to be President," continued Mrs. Madigan. "Oh! worra, worra, sorra the day that thief of a gypsy crossed yer path; what devilment is she up to now anyhow?" she said, as she disappeared behind the curtains, following the maid to the door.

"Ah, the Irish fraulein. It is not good. It is the same with man—women, women, always women, eh? Herr Waldie?"

"By all the curses! Paulina go, before I lose my temper. You have brought sorrow enough upon me and my house. You and I now, in the one room, are not safe," he said rather excitedly.

"Good! Good!" said Paulina, gleefully, "I love the tiger; look! look! ah!"

"Not content with bleeding me time and time again for sums in no way due you, you must frighten my wife—oh, you she-devil, you scum of the earth, you—"

"Ha, ha! Continue. It is glorious. My son-in-law! Come, why not strike immediate; it is good! See this marriage certificate?"

"The paper I paid you for gone! And you are the only one who could have taken it, for you saw me put it there when I paid you. This paper you must show my wife, you fiend; you should be burned in oil."

"No; for the moment I am a man, a devil; what you will; strike! I wish it."

"For three years, yes four, I have tried to blot out the past, to repair the wrong, to live a different life, to—"

"Words, words, mere words; if the truth, if not married to Naomi, why not marry her?"

"Merciful God! Woman, are you crazy?"

"No, Herr Waldie is tired of his plaything—she who lives on his every word, whose child bears his face, his smile, his eye, aye his frown. My God! One rule for the women, and the flexible, pliable one for the man, his own pleasure. The eternal God say the Herr Waldie shall be crushed by this little hand."

"Then know, Paulina, that I have told my wife all; that from this day I shall be a new man, with new associates, new hopes, new ambitions. Your form must never darken these doors again. Now go; I have paid you well; never trouble me again. I will take care of Naomi and the child—but you, never, never," he said, leaving her abruptly.

"The gentle fraulein have forgiven!" continued Paulina to herself. "Um, the sting was not deep enough. Poor, silly fool. And for a man! Ah! woman, woman, you the clinging vine; man the trunk with thorns, and when he tear you away you still reach up to him, still cling, bleeding, oh, so fast, till all your life is gone. But I—No, I am not that weak, silly fool. It is complete. Bart Waldie has made it final. He shall not live now. I care not for God or devils—it is all one; all one. Naomi, my child! I have lived for Nature's vengeance. It is complete; one touch, one sip, and he is dead. Hush! No, no one see me. Herr Waldie I go, and when I see you in the coffin I spit on you. I curse you, the gypsy's oath, Paulina's curse."

With a hasty glance about she had taken a glass from the table, filled it with water from the pitcher and put in liquid from a small vial in her bosom; then putting the glass near the papers on the desk, she was just about to fill the glass when Jasper entered, deeply absorbed in a book. His attention was arrested by the action of Paulina, and he stood aside till Paulina left the room; then took the glass, sniffed it, threw the water out, called to Susan, "Susan, wash that glass in boiling water," and then he calmly went on reading his book.

Bart returned shortly after to see if Paulina had gone, and he had now fallen into a habit of talking to himself, as old men do in their dotage or as those in deep trouble.

"For a week past I have had shooting pains about the heart, and this last interview with Paulina has unnerved me. I am weak, faint, where is that glass? Susan; where is my glass?"

Susan came in with the glass. "Mr. Juniper told me to wash it out with boiling water. I'll bring it."

"With boiling water? Oh, some fancy of his about drinking our city water. Thank you, Susan, you may go. If my life were written—" continued Bart, "what a warning it would hold to young men; begun wrongly, ending disastrously; for I feel my end is coming and coming quickly. What have I to leave Agnes but a shattered life, a dishonored name, a wasted fortune? That letter must be written at once. History repeats itself. There is the rise, the floating on the wave of success, the downfall—Warwick, Wolsey, Macbeth, Boss Tweed—the whole lot of them. I don't feel well enough to go down town to-day. McCutcheon must see the boys for me."

He went to the telephone and told him to come to the house, as he was going to quit politics; and it did not take long for the news to spread.

"What is it to be a successful politician—the futile following of the will o' the wisp," continued Bart to himself; "modern politics is not a business, a trade, a profession—it is the bloody work of a parasite, a relentless leech—a cruel dragon." Then he began writing a letter, continuing his talking. "Clean politics— as well call sewers murmuring mountain brooks. There, Agnes, you will know the one shut-up secret of my life, the one skeleton in my house—to be opened when you may marry again, when I am dead! Agnes, my wife, my love," he said, kissing his wife when she came toward him.

"Lunch is ready, dear; what are you writing?"

"No matter now. I do not feel well enough for lunch. Excuse me to everybody."

"I will send you a cup of tea."

"No; I expect McCutcheon here in a few minutes. I will come later."

"Come as soon as you can," said Agnes, going.

A few minutes later McCutcheon and Schledgmilch were in the room.

"Boss, how you vas? I was mit Jimmy when you rung him up; so I come along," said the German, with his familiar asthmatic wheeze.

"What's the muss, old man? You're white about the gills. Who's given you the cold shake?" inquired Mc-Cutcheon.

"The papers says you'll be detained in office. The old cocks of the ward have ruffled feathers. There is too much limburger in the air. Now, a little subscription from the Boss," said Schledgmilch, with his familiar old wink.

With eyes fixed on the floor and in vacancy, as if not listening to these men, Bart announced: "Gentlemen, I shall withdraw from active politics at the close of my term—perhaps immediately," he concluded, starting up suddenly.

"What?" was the exclamation from both at once.

"I am tired of continually striving after something thoroughly unsatisfactory when you get it," continued Bart.

"Well, not much you don't, until we've divided the swag. There's two offices for me; wine, carriages and sundries for the boys."

"Four offices for me; the dry goods account for my frau; Madame Porteo and her flock."

"And a few decks of workers dead to rights, when I gets the spots," rejoined McCutcheon.

"Yah! You don't walk out and leave us mit the empty bag."

"Not much you don't. You're on the pious lay to-day."

"Where is the man who preaches, get money, get it honestly if you can; if you can't why get it, eh? Don't it?" chuckled Schledgmilch.

"Gentlemen, leave my house at once," broke in Bart; "never speak to me again; it is you and such as you who have ruined me, wrecked me and my life."

"Oh, yes; a good wreck on a $10,000 salary. Come, divy up, old man; shell out," insisted McCutcheon with a greedy grin

"How much?" inquired Bart indifferently.

"Four thousand apiece."

"That's too much."

"Ah, now with that story of Naomi and the child," threatened Schledgmilch.

"Nice in cold print, eh, Gottlieb?" said McCutcheon, punching his pal in the rib.

"Yah, and the crooked work at Springfield last winter."

"Four blank checks to bearer," insinuated McCutcheon.

"Not to-day; I will do what is right; my word is good, my record is clear."

"Oh, yes, where did your swell home come from?"

"Mac, do you know to whom you are talking?"

"Yes; Bart Waldie mit the clean record; down on Clark street. Yah!" rejoined the German.

"Gentlemen, you can neither frighten me nor move me. I have made up my mind to face the issue. Tell what you please."

"Well, we won't quit cold. You keep your promise or we will make you—you treacherous hound," said McCutcheon, suddenly coming toward him with a threatening look.

"Yes, the old man is a dead dog if he barks mit this shicken."

"I have always stuck by my friends, and you are both ungrateful curs, whom I have paid, overpaid, many times over; now I propose to be my own master, devote my time to my home and wife."

"We thought Naomi—" sneered McCutcheon.

This was too much. Bart rushed, staggering toward them.

"Move quick or by God! You are both infernal cowards, born of the slums, the dregs of earth, jail-birds, thieves, parasites—move quick—quick, I say— Oh Agnes! My head! My head! I—I—"

With a deathly moan Bart fell into the chair. Both eyes were fixed in the ghastly stare of death. The excitement had resulted in a fatal stroke of apoplexy.

Schledgmilch, with pistol drawn, and McCutcheon, with knife in his hand, realized the horrible truth.

Bart Waldie's last summons had come.

CHAPTER XXVIII.

"Even children followed with endearing wile."
                                        —Goldsmith.
"Where humble happiness endeared each scene."
                                        —Goldsmith.

When Agnes returned to Poplarville, she found that during her absence her enemies had been busy. Friendships often do not seem to wear well unless the principals are very much *en evidence,* The school board had employed a substitute, and had concluded in the meantime to dispense with her services, especially since it was said that she was the "divorced wife of a Chicago boss politician." It was felt that "her influence on the children might not be the best." . This decision raised a tumult among the pupils, but the elders with wise looks declared they knew best, and when Agnes returned she found she had been dismissed. It was a hard blow, but her life had been so thoroughly tempered to misfortune that, although her hair was turning gray, she still maintained that sweet and determined spirit.

The new order of things had been precipitated in the village school. When Agnes first went to Poplarville, a young girl of eighteen, she inaugurated the breaking loose from the old district school idea, but that was some years ago. Now the new era had been pretty firmly established. The purpose of developing original, self-reliant personalities was replaced by object lessons—a made-easy method of instruction. The teacher was given so many pupils to grind out in a proper manner. Pretty little forms were provided to facilitate a well-organized thinking machine. Discipline and Delsarte were two ideals of perfection. Cram, stuff and specialize the thinking machines was the order of the day, and Agnes, not having been altogether in touch with the last "institute," she was declared behind the times.

The pupils would have openly rebelled and gone out on a strike had she not been there to pacify them. They loved her, and when she talked to them they desisted.

She was then staying with Elbert's mother, who was very indignant over the matter, and wrote Elbert in Washington all about it. Agnes was about to leave Poplarville and look elsewhere for a school to earn a livelihood, when a telegram was received.

"Have Mrs. Waldie remain. Letter to follow. Elbert."

A few days later Elbert himself arrived from Washington. Life in the capital city had been wearisome to him, and he was always anxious for a pretext to come home and see baby Veo. After they had talked over Bart's sad death, he broke in:

"Now, I have a plan," said Elbert. "Veo is almost three years old, and she can only have one teacher according to my wish—and that is the one who did so much for her father."

"But, Elbert, I cannot be a pensioner," objected Agnes.

"Very true, Mrs. Proud Lady, but now let me finish. Kindergartens are a new thing in this section; use a portion of mother's house and inaugurate the idea, with little Veo as your first pupil."

"A splendid plan, Elbert," said his mother enthusiastically.

"But teaching little children is all new to me," she remonstrated.

"Well, human beings are all built on the same plan," said Elbert, as if finally settling the question.

Elbert went even farther with his advice. Being a keen observer, he realized the existing influences which politeness often forbids mentioning even in a whisper. Active church work he believed had its commercial value. A social position is rarely attained without growth, and the person who sits modestly in a dark corner, waiting to be discovered is very liable to be overlooked. He believed in energy in one's own behalf, and urged Agnes to throw off her inclination to exclusiveness.

"You owe your talents to society, and besides—besides—it's business," said Elbert.

"But it is inconsistent that all my·talents should bloom forth so suddenly when my work depends upon public favor."

"No matter. These social influences are simply irresistible in religious, commercial, political or professional careers."

Elbert's advice prevailed, and the tact of Agnes for organization and her personal attractions came into good play. She organized entertainments to be pro-

duced for the benefit of the public library, and this
brought her in close touch with the young people and
the musicians of the community. The "Thursday Club,"
which she later organized, included a large membership
of mothers, and was of a semi-literary and semi-social
nature. Her little talks on home life attracted them to
her, and they were unconsciously led to appreciate her
capabilities as a kindergarten instructor. The "Mite
Societies" always looked to her to devise some new
form of social entertainment. In a church choir she
was the proverbial peacemaker, and held together the
soapbubble elements which so frequently threatened
collapse. In fact, she worked incessantly in a semi-
public way, and her kindergarten at once flourished as
one of the indirect results. Her devoted attachment
to little Veo seemed to generate an affection for the
other little ones, and as she watched their characters
unfold day by day she grew to love them and her work
passionately. While naturally she had many jealous
critics, her unassuming modesty and transcendent
worth brought her a supreme social triumph in Poplarville. She had calmly ignored the petty flings of
jealous enemies, and her sweet manner and common
sense thoroughly disarmed her assailants. The touch
of pathetic history and her personal sorrow seemed
to stimulate the general esteem in which she was now
held.

"Yes, my life is now settled among these little flowers," she reflected, as the children crowded about her.

"Mamma Aggie is so dood," said little Veo, climbing
into her lap and putting a rose into her teacher's hair.

And the tear that Agnes quickly brushed away was not altogether one of sorrow.

Jasper, who happened to be passing, seeing the little ones at their play, thought he would drop in for a word of encouragement, and leave a mysterious parcel for Mary Jane, who insisted on doing the "dustin' and sweepin'" for Agnes.

Little Veo rushed to Jasper as he entered, and took off his spectacles and put them on, with mock gravity.

"Who does Veo love best?" he asked.

"Mamma Aggie."

"Ah, tut, tut, tut, who brings you candy when papa is away?"

"Uncle Jasper."

"Well, who do you love best?"

"Mamma Aggie."

"You dear little soul; well love Mamma Aggie best; we all do."

"Yes, there's something to live for in this world besides the accumulation of wealth and making gingerbread," broke in Mary Jane, vigorously dusting the room. "Snakes, how's the fire?"

"Good, ma'am, I'm learnin' teacher, I am. Mother's dead, but I told her last night I'm happy," said the poor girl, coming in slowly as little Veo and Agnes went out.

"Mary Jane, I am inclined to be sad and poetic today," said Jasper, deliberately crossing his legs.

"Have some sense, Jasper; don't let the wheel of fortune make a fool of you," said Mary Jane in a consoling way.

"Yes, I know, Mary Jane, but we are getting old. I thought that when we died it would be a good idea to have our bones laid away together."

"Jasper Juniper," said Mary Jane, with a flourish of the duster, "do you suppose I want any post mortem wedding?" and she left the room with a flounce.

"Well, I must be movin'. You are happy here, Agnes, I hope," said Jasper, somewhat flustrated, as if trying to relieve the awkward situation, when Agnes met him at the door.

"Oh, yes, very happy. Every spot about the dear old place awakens such tender memories. Mrs. Ainsworth was a mother to me when I came here years ago, an orphan girl. The trees are friends, the birds, the flowers. True, faces are older, but memories are young."

"Yes, I think we owe the progress of our village to those new ideas you instilled into the school years ago. But I must be going over the river before noon," continued Jasper. "Agnes, you are giving them children a long recess. Veo, come here and give your Uncle Jasper a good rousing smack: how do the shoes fit?"

"All yight, all yight," she said, giving him a quizzical look.

"You little midge; you are a second edition of your mother. Now wink that eye as your mother did. Ha! ha! She's Veo all over again. Here, let my tails alone; let go I say; that's just the trick her mother had, Agnes. Let go, I say, you witch, there's no candy there. Now you can't catch me," he said, as he ran around the kindergarten table and stumbled and fell. Veo put her arms about his neck, and he got up and went out with the child on his shoulder, calling back, "There's nothing like this in Plutarch's Lives."

When the bell tapped the children rushed into the house, while Mary Jane, seated at a piano, painfully picked out the chords of a simple march as the children formed a procession to take their seats.

They had just completed the opening song when Abner and "Snakes" appeared at the door and looked upon the happy scene.

CHAPTER XXIX.

"Solid men of Boston, banish long potations;
Solid men of Boston, make no long orations."
—American Song, Charles Morris.

Elbert's Washington life had been fruitful in furthering his cherished ambitions. His first year's seclusion had now become rather irksome, only broken by his frequent visits home to see little Veo. On one of the nights of soberest reflection, when his mind and body were overcome with weariness, he became restless and felt the spirit of discontent creeping over him. He had received an invitation from Mrs. W. Dannocks Daniels to a dinner on the following evening at her home, F street N. W. The invitation was a surprise, as he had not heard of her directly since they parted at Bart's home, and he was now debating as to whether or not he should accept the invitation. Veo's picture on the mantel was his oracle, and the bright eyes seemed to speak to him, saying, "Go, Elbert, don't throw away your life in sorrow; I am happy." He had begun to feel keenly the social ostracism of a Congressman, and accepted the invitation. He found a delightful little dinner party assembled at the home of Mrs. Daniels, and among them a number of acquaintances, relieving him from the awkwardness of feeling an absolute stranger. Mrs. Daniels gave him a warm welcome.

"Why have you so buried yourself? I arrived home nearly a year ago, and you have not had the courtesy to call," said the hostess with one of her sweetest smiles.

"I must apologize, but Mrs. Daniels—"

"Let me see; it is now Congressman Ainsworth, I believe."

"Yes, your opposition to my political career has borne fruit."

"Just like a man, stubborn and inconsistent. But then, I congratulate you," she said, extending her hand.

"Perhaps you had better wait until I have won in the congressional joust."

"Well, I shall not think less of you as a congressman, but you know Washington society is graded in this way. Congressmen, clerks and niggers."

"Well, I have moved up a notch, anyhow," he said, laughing, "and I may yet reach your social level."

"Mr. Ainsworth, how cruel of you; I did not mean that to be a reflection in any way."

"I know it, but you see new congressmen are especially sensitive as to their social standing."

"Well now, what is your first plan?" she said, as they sat down together.

"To fix matters for a re-election. My lamented predecessor has borne the brunt of the fight in the distribution of post offices and patronage, and—"

"Perhaps that is what killed the poor fellow," she suggested. "Seriously, the distribution of offices is the great wearing and tearing problem to the modern statesman."

"Well, I have but very few poor relations, and few political pals to care for."

"There will be enough of them, and you will realize that a congressional career is not all a bed of roses, but now, since you are a congressman, you must be my gallant knight in the political tournament."

"Surely you are not seeking political office or political honors, Mrs. Daniels?"

"Oh, no; but then I love excitement, and while political combat is just now at a low ebb I am not going to desert you."

"What is my first duty?"

"To make a hit," she said, decisively. "Watch your opportunity, and ignite a blaze of eloquence; let others drudge for the committee honors."

The advice of Mrs. Daniels he considered important, and at once made a collection of all his Memorial Day addresses and Fourth of July speeches which had blazed with the patriotic metaphors of ardent youth. As the son of a Union soldier, he had written them with a degree of sincerity, and cultivated catch phrases, word painting and striking alliterations that would put a newspaper heading to shame.

But with all his preparation the opportunity did not seem in a hurry to present itself. He felt that his congressional career was decidedly empty of new-born honors. Towards the close of the session, while sitting in his seat reading a newspaper carelessly and perplexed as to how to adjust the requests of constituents for seeds, he was awakened from his lethargy. A bill was under consideration for an appropriation to beautify a soldiers' cemetery. A Southern member had made some slighting remarks with reference to Union soldiers which made Elbert's blood tingle. The bill was to come up for final consideration the following day. He at once looked up the chairman in charge of the bill, and requested that he be allowed a portion of the time allotted for its discussion, and it was granted rather grudgingly. That night he plunged into the work of preparing his maiden speech.

The next day the time was yielded to him and he began.

There was the usual buzz and indifference that greets all except the few noted speakers in the House, and even the speaker's gavel and admonitions failed to establish quiet. "The gentlemen in the aisles will please be seated," roared the speaker again. Elbert raised his voice above the tumult. There are some voices that always attract attention, but it was Elbert's first speech, and it took some time for even his rich, resonant voice to penetrate the confusion. Quiet was gradually restored and Elbert had hearing. He lost himself in speaking, and his lurid word pictures at first occasioned an inclination to smile amongst his older and more incredulous colleagues. His theme was one in which words could be spoken in a thrilling and dramatic way, and were even of more importance than ideas. When his time was nearly up, the members began to exclaim from all parts of the house, "Go on, go on," and the speaker announced an extension of time. Elbert had exhausted his set speech, and it was a crisis with him, as he was at a loss to know what to say further. The applause in the galleries had been terrific, as if they were anxious to do honor to a newly discovered favorite. Elbert glanced toward a private gallery, and saw the face of Mrs. Daniels. She was enthusiastically applauding. The glance was an inspiration, and the words and phrases of his old Memorial Day address came flooding back to his memory, and for thirty minutes he held the hearers spell-bound. The stenographers rushed about, and followed him with note books in hand as he paced excitedly up and down the aisles.

When he had concluded the applause was tremendous, and the newspapers heralded Elbert Ainsworth as a rising political star, and his speech was a refreshing departure from the hum-drum routine of the House. A large number of his colleagues crowded about his seat to congratulate him, and as he left the House chamber he met Mrs. Daniels in the corridor.

"Mr. Ainsworth, you have won your laurels and I am proud of you," she said, pressing his hand.

"I am so glad you were here," he said, candidly.

"When I read last night you were to speak I felt that the opportunity had come," she replied.

He accepted her invitation to a dinner party feeling quite contented with himself.

While Elbert did not attend any state military balls or mingle in the big S set, he found in Mrs. Daniels a charming friend. With a man's usual egotism he imagined the dinners were given for his especial pleasure by her, and that she was truly his affinity in the discussion of literature, art and music. Amateur cultured parlor musicians after all are the ones who appreciate the worth of music. They feel a deeper soul in harmony, because unable to render the work of the masters with professional finish. To the professional, music is in part a task; and while their efforts may please and reach the real heights, it is the responsive sympathy of the amateur musicians which forms the basis of their artistic success.

"It is as great an accomplishment to appreciatively listen to and comprehend music as to render it," said Mrs. Daniels one evening when she and Elbert were having an hour of music together.

He had been regretting the fact that he had not studied music in early life, and she had just finished singing the "Evening Song," from Tannhauser.

"Why is it I never enjoy a Wagner opera? Il Trovatore always appeals to me as real music," said Elbert.

"Because you have a false idea of the real mission of opera. Wagner revives the old Greek idea—opera is the musical expression of dramatic art. It is not a thread of sickly concert hall ballads and vocal embroidery to please the ear palate; that is not dramatic expression. No; there is that deeper, subtler language of the soul—too sacred for hackneyed barrel organ arias—it is music not merely to please, but to express and uplift."

"Yes, music is the language of heaven," continued Elbert. "You are right; words cannot express the passions and feelings that music makes clear; and, Mrs. Daniels, somehow when you sing the words and sentiment sparkle in a new light from their meaning in ordinary conversation."

He did not exactly mean it as an expression of sentiment toward her, but it sounded very much that way. Mrs. Daniels continued singing with all the passionate earnestness of an amateur musician. The "Swan Song," from Lohengrin, seemed to enrapture Elbert with its plaintive and almost inexpressible yearning. When she had concluded, he said:

"It seems as if some composers had attuned every note and syllable to a responsive chord in the human heart."

"Yes," she replied, "each composer seems to have a particular favorite key in which to express certain emotions."

"But the emotion of love seems to run the entire gamut, doesn't it?"

She answered with a few improvised chords on the piano.

They said good-bye that night in a gentler and more reserved manner than usual.

Naturally the gossips began to talk about Elbert's frequent visits, and society newspapers hinted as to the coming nuptials of the widow of a well known army officer and a rising young congressman. Elbert heard of it, but ignored it, feeling that he had found a dear friend in the tourist companion of former years, and continued fluttering about the flame.

A few evenings later Elbert sat in Mrs. Daniels' parlor, sighing as to the loneliness of his bachelor quarters. He had not forgotten the old trick of assuming a heroic attitude, although he insisted that he had no inclination to be a genius if he had to go through with all the grief and sorrow that their biographies record.

"I sometimes think that I am growing almost purposeless in life, Mrs. Daniels."

"That is wrong," said Mrs. Daniels, with a quizzical look in her jet black eyes. "You need not be so frightfully alone," she continued, half blushing and looking down.

He pretended not to see the point and went on blindly:

"But who would care to—"

"Elbert, why do you persist in shutting your eyes?"

This was a pretty declaration for Mrs. Daniels and he was fascinated with her. He looked straight into her eyes for that soul response which the love message from Veo had given him. It was not there.

Bidding her good-night, he left Mrs. Daniels more precipitately than gracefully.

CHAPTER XXX.

"And the heart that is soonest awake to the flowers,
Is always the first to be touched ·by the thorns."
                                                    —Moore.

As Elbert passed down Fifteenth street on his way
home that night he was very much agitated. He had
spent his life in analyzing others, but had overlooked
himself. There was a hidden happiness in the thought
that he was loved. All human beings desire to be loved;
but could he marry again, and did he love Mrs. Daniels? That was the question. There was certainly not
the same feeling toward her which he had felt for Veo.
Mrs. Daniels was beautiful, intellectual and inspirational—"A good match," as the gossips say—and he
was attracted to her, yes, fascinated. Yet, when his
yearning heart searched for that simple soul glance
of Veo it was not there, and he felt that something was
lacking. He wrote a hurried note to Mrs. Daniels and
left the very next day for Poplarville. There are some
things in which the most scrupulously candid and honest men will deceive themselves, and like all human beings, Elbert's actions and ideals were often illogical
and inconsistent. He was not a coward, and yet he
felt that he could not trust himself with Mrs. Daniels
longer until he thoroughly knew his own heart. The
memory of their various conversations at Brussels and
at Bart's home came back vividly. If she tired of one

husband, why not another. It was a struggle with him all the way home.

There was something soothing in the quiet atmosphere of Poplarville after the distracting bustle of Washington life, and his unexpected arrival was quite a surprise.

"And my little Veo doesn't know papa?"

"'Es I do, but 'oo look so sorry, papa," said the little girl in a searching way.

There was in the child's face the old tender, sympathetic look of Veo.

Later on Agnes came in. She seemed more radiantly beautiful than ever. Her whitening hair and blooming cheeks made a striking contrast. Her voice, gentle and low, yet firm and decisive.

"Oh, mamma, I's so happy," and little Veo left her father to go to her teacher as she entered.

"Elbert, I must thank you for your advice and assistance; it has quite made a new woman of me."

"Not a real new woman, I hope," he said in mock surprise.

"Oh, no," she replied, laughing, "but with these children life is so sweet and refreshing. I believe being with them is making an elderly person young again."

"Now, don't talk of being an elderly person yet."

"As your school teacher I have a right to expect you to respect my age," she said, laughing.

That evening they were sitting alone together on the veranda.

"I have something to tell you," said Elbert, soberly. "I have come home again for advice."

"Well, as your old teacher, take your seat and confess," said Agnes, pointing to a kindergarten seat.

"Indeed and it is serious; do you remember this Mrs. Daniels?"

"Perfectly; I have cause to."

"She entertains famously at Washington and has contributed to my success; I have been frequently at her home and matters have become serious without my knowing it. She has made a direct proposal and I don't know what to do."

"'Um! a woman's privilege, the year is divisible by four—leap year."

"It came upon me like a shock; I ran away—ran out of the house most unceremoniously without a word."

"You were always a peculiar boy; Bart and I sometimes thought you rarely understood women."

"Perhaps so; what shall I do, tell me honestly?"

"Do you love her?"

"Well, no; not exactly; something seems to hold me back; her audacity has shocked me, and yet—"

"There is only one answer then; let your heart speak that—"

"My heart? It is laid away with Veo yonder. Yet Mrs. Daniels is brilliant—"

"Think it over, Elbert, and your heart will—"

"My heart says no."

"Then be true to your heart."

She turned to him in the pale moonlight as she said these words, laying her hand on his arm and giving him that soul-expressive and trusting look in her deep blue eyes, that seemed to reflect memories of his heart's first love. It fired him with a suddenly awakened impulse.

"This moment it has spoken, Agnes, my heart, Agnes!" he uttered in a voice quivering with emotion, as he started to draw her to him.

"Elbert, Elbert, what do you mean? You surely forget," she said, as she drew away with queenly dignity.

"Forgive me, Agnes, but your eyes just now taught me my heart. Crush me—but heaven only knows that you are the only woman I could ever love again."

"Elbert, you must be rational. I, your old school teacher, your friend? I, who loved Veo—why, reason, Elbert."

"Reason with love? As well reason with a whirlwind. Agnes, it may be wrong to say this to you, but I cannot help it, and in you only can I hope for solace and comfort in life since—"

Agnes had turned very pale, and stood plucking the leaves from the vine which clambered up the veranda where they were standing. She felt as if she had betrayed confidence and stolen love that was not intended.

"Elbert, you will say no more about this," she said, turning to him. "It pains me; let me continue your friend."

"Agnes, it is yours to command," he said resignedly. "Perhaps I chose a foolish time; perhaps my words lack fiery eloquence; but you told me to let my heart decide and my heart has spoken."

The events naturally caused a more reserved attitude between them during the remainder of Elbert's visit, and the scene on the veranda was not referred to by either of them afterwards. When Agnes was putting little Veo to bed that night she said:

"Mamma Aggie, 'oo loves papa, don't 'oo?"

"Yes, dear," she said, stroking her hair.

"Mamma Aggie will never go away from little Veo, will she?"

Agnes kissed her for an answer, and little Veo repeated her usual prayer: "Dear Dod, bless mamma in heaven; bless papa—bless—Mamma Aggie, 'oo's crying; I's so sorry," said little Veo, looking up suddenly.

"Finish your prayer, little one," said Agnes, with a reassuring smile.

CHAPTER XXXI.

"Revenge, at first thought sweet,
Bitter ere long back on itself recoils."
—Milton.

Poplarville had gone a long time without having a real sensational event when Shandy Goff introduced bicycles. And it was indeed a disturbing element, and the community was especially shocked when Mary Jane Toots calmly announced that she was going to learn to ride the wheel.

"Now that I have bought it, land o' Goshen, I have got to ride it," she explained.

"Come, Mary Jane, I am ready for that spin over the river," said Shandy, peering in at the door.

"I am so flustrated I don't really know whether I am standing on my head or my heels. It's like taking the first plunge in swimming. Which foot do I put on first?" she cried, as she tried to get on the wheel, Shandy holding her, and it made a truly comic scene.

The news soon spread over the village that Shandy was teaching Mary Jane to ride a bicycle, and while they were practicing Abner and Jasper came up to witness the excitement.

"Just as I expected," growled Abner. "The devil's uppermost in Poplarville to-day. No religion, no veneration, no politics, no nothin' that's got any sense in it."

"Just the other way," cried Shandy, pumping up his tire. "Everything has grown better except you and the old fossils."

"There, there, what did I tell you, you young calamity spinner; wastin' good muscle on that darn thing instead of plowin' your land."

"Bicycles are all right, Abner," said Jasper. "Shandy, let Abner try."

"Me try! I'd sooner get on the devil's broom stick and ride to hell than touch the pesky critter; ruining the oat crops these bicycles are."

"Mary Jane, I can't get reconciled to these bloomers," said Jasper. "Now for the Turks it might be all right, but—"

"Well, you must submit, I suppose; always said so," said Dr. Buzzer, coming up.

"I'm simply following the edicts of hygiene and Fowler on Common Sense," she said, with a sarcastic bow to Jasper.

"She's got you there, Jasper," said the doctor, laughing.

"I don't propose to get killed by any skirts getting around my legs, like that woman in St. Louis the other day," said Mary Jane, as she zig-zagged off like a drunken kite.

"Well, you'd better go to Turkey, seein' that ye want to do as them Turkeys do," hollered Abner after her.

"There's a verse in Plutarch that fits the case—"

"Oh, Uncle Jasper, bicycles in Rome? You're a trifle off your history," protested Shandy.

"You're both fit for circus clowns; better hire to

onst. They pay good wages, so I'm told," said Abner in his usual gruff way.

"Come, Mary Jane, let's go for another spin," said Shandy, as she came back to try it again.

"Yes, ride to the devil why don't you?" snarled Abner, as the two started off.

"Abner, it's no use; we must keep pace with the times, the improvements of the age," said the doctor, as "Snakes" came in hurriedly.

"Doctor, my head hurts so—I—mother's dead," she said, as she fell suddenly forward.

Jasper lifted her up and examined her face. She had fallen in a dead faint, striking her head against the edge of the stoop. Jasper went for water. The doctor lifted her up, felt her pulse, examined her face, and saw her eyes fixed and staring.

They carried the prostrate form into the house, laying her upon a lounge, when the doctor made a careful examination.

"Compression of the skull, eh?" said the doctor, examining her head with care. "What's this? An old scar, depression of the skull. Damnation, some foul play here."

At this time Abner broke in.

"Oh, let the critter go. It is nothing; always had those spells when she was young."

"Abner, you know something about this case."

"I? Oh, no."

The doctor had opened his instrument case, and taking out scissors, scalpal and trepan, cut away "Snakes'" hair.

"Well, I'll quickly find out," he said, working away with the instruments, laying bare the skull. He found the inner table of the skull depressed.

"There, now, we will see what we will see," he said, as he gently bathed Snakes' face and head. "Look, Abner, into her eyes. I have simply raised the inner table of the skull which has been causing pressure on the brain and made poor Snakes crazy."

"No, thank ye."

"Do as the doctor says, Abner," said Jasper, watching intently the unconscious girl.

As Snakes slowly regained consciousness and saw Abner, she seemed to speak rationally.

"Take him away; he did it; Uncle Abner, I'll be a good girl. I know you, Doctor. Brother Bart went to Chicago yesterday."

"Brother Bart!" exclaimed Jasper.

"Brother Bart said he would send for me when I was ten years old."

"Ten years old! That was fifteen years ago," said the doctor.

"Tell us, Abner, what all this means, or by the Eternal, I'll put you under lock and key," said Jasper, who still felt his dignity as justice.

"Ye can't; I've done nothing."

"Speak man," urged the doctor.

"Well, it's not a long story and I know you like gossip. She's Bart's half-sister. That's true. Bart's mother gave me the mitten and sneered at me as her father's hired man, and I swore vengeance. She married the other fellow. This child was born over in Pike County, Indiana. I stole it from the mother in a fit of passion when she was six years old. I told Bart she was dead. The mother believed me. I kept her until she was eight, then got frightened. A doctor over the river said he would fix her for me if I wanted her out of the way. I was not quite the villain for that, so he said he'd take her senses from her. He did. You doctors are great chaps, anyway."

"And so he opened the skull and put this pressure on the brain. He trepanned and depressed where I have elevated. Poor Snakes! Poor Snakes!" said the doctor, shaking his head.

"That was when you put her on the county, eh? Abner—get out. I give you one hour to get bail or kill yourself. I told you to get $3,000 bail for mal-treatment and cruelty. No wonder you—you—there's nothing in Plutarch to fit this case," said Jasper in a fury.

"Ye can't; ye can't; she's got her senses now and ye can't do nothing."

"We'll see; Abner come with me. Come, I said," said Jasper, authoritatively.

"I tell ye, ye can't," exclaimed Abner, hobbling off with him.

"I'm so happy, doctor, I don't understand it," said Snakes faintly. "Yet I seem to know something— mother, yes, mother must be dead. They killed her, but it seems so awful—"

"Yes, child, now rest quiet and take care of yourself; you may have a happy life yet."

Of course the whole story was soon known in the village, and created a feeling against Abner, which he realized and was discreet enough to leave the country quietly that night.

CHAPTER XXXII.

"Oh! my offense is rank, it smells to heaven,
It has the primal, eldest curse upon't,
A brother's murder."

—Hamlet.

The even tenor of life at the Poplarville kindergarten was resumed after Elbert left. His visits always interfered to some extent with the general schedule, as Agnes desired to show him in various ways the progress made. Gradually she found herself preparing for his visits with pleasurable anticipation, and his approval quite naturally pleased her. The "Snakes" sensation was told in various ways, and Dr. Buzzer was the hero of the hour, with the village gossips.

That day little Veo, with the spirit of inquisitiveness characteristic of children, while left alone by Agnes in her room, began to rummage the desk. She was looking for paper dolls, and one of her childish delights was to open sealed letters when her grandpa brought them. She had seen her father do it, and felt it quite an honor when he asked her to open his letters. She found a letter in the drawer unopened and proceeded to break the envelope. Finding still others, her busy little hands continued, and the drawer fell out, overturning the entire contents on the floor. Just then Agnes came in.

"Why, Veo, what are you doing?"

"Mamma Aggie, don't scold, I was des busy, and it tipped up itself. I's so sorry."

"But, my little Veo must be more careful."

"Is Mamma Aggie so sorry?"

"Yes, dear. Give me the letters and I'll put them away, and then run and have grandma get you ready for bed."

She kissed the sweet little face as Veo put up her lips for a token of forgiveness.

Agnes then stooped to pick up the remainder of the papers, and among them she caught sight of a letter in Bart's handwriting. She thought it strange that it should be there, and yet it awakened old memories. After putting away the remainder of the packages, she started to read the letter by the light of the fire. It was that hour after twilight when we linger in reveries of the past. The heading startled her:

Her heart almost stopped beating as she read on:

"Agnes, forgive me; it was not the blow of a murderer, but a stroke of love—love for you, Agnes; but that love was never returned. When you read this I will be lying in my grave beside Wesley, with no other monument than an accursed life."

Was she dreaming? No. She read on:

"I did not want my death secret to disturb you until you were again married and in a happy home, where you were loved and returned that love. The night before your wedding was to occur I met Wesley in the office. He was radiantly happy in your love, and was counting the money and drafts, which we had neglected to deposit that day. I stood back of him looking over his shoulder, and a wild, maddening impulse came upon me suddenly and I struck him upon the head with an ink bottle—the fatal blow. It was not a blow of hate, but love. I loved Wesley and my grief in his death was sincere. I had no impulse to conceal the murder, and simply walked away and left him dead with the thought that you would now love me. Oh, it is maddening to recall that night, and yet I seemed then dead to all remorse for the murderous act. It did not seem as if my hand had killed him, but that it was the hand of Providence. Not one minute's meditation was given for the deed. I did not even conceive of the tragical consequences. With the stained hands of Cain I sought to woo you, and won your gratitude, which replaced your love. Oh, Agnes, I dare not ask for pity and forgiveness, and yet I knew not what I did. No human lips could justify the deed, but when I am dead, accursed with a wrecked life and sleeping the sleep of a murderer, you may pity. I write this knowing that my end is near. The future is blank, but death is sweet relief from the hell I have suffered all these years, even in the light of your smile.

"BART."

Her impulse was to read it again, thinking it a frightful dream. One more look at the signature—no, it was true. Like a flash she opened the stove door and the story of Bart Waldie's crime was burned, and yet even on the charred and burned papers the words of his confession remained quite distinct.

"Even fire does not destroy the blackness of that

crime. Oh, Wesley! Wesley!" she cried on her knees before the fire. "Noble Wesley! Love of my youth! Sacrificed to an ingrate brother's passion!" It was the crowning grief that seemed to tear her very heart-strings.

"Why have I to suffer so much? Oh, Lord, teach me to endure and bear my burdens in patience."

The knowledge of Bart's crime hung over her like a pall.

"How can I ever meet Elbert again?" she moaned.

CHAPTER XXXIII.

"For taking the year altogether, my dear,
There's never more night than day."

-Holmes.

Grief and worry always demand a penalty, and Agnes was taken very ill after the terrible revelation in Bart's letter. Her life was despaired of, but Dr. Buzzer insisted "That girl's got the grit to pull through, by ginger." In her delirium Agnes had said things which set the tongues of the gossips to wagging. Dr. Buzzer made a heroic attempt to stem the tide of talk by giving out various sufficient causes of her illness, but the difficulty was that all of his various reasons did not precisely agree, and the doctor found things growing worse than if he had said nothing at all. Just an inkling of the real truth began to leak out, but it was also hinted that Agnes had attempted to take her life.

When she was convalescent, but a mere shadow of her former self, she heard of Elbert's coming to Poplarville.

"Ask him to remain away—until I am better," was her request to his mother.

"Why, Agnes, what is the matter? Nothing could keep Elbert away at such a time as this."

Agnes' reply was a deep sigh.

Elbert was at her bedside the next day, and she implored him to go away.

"Agnes, you need not fear my alluding to the scenes of the last visit if it pains you, but I am your friend and protector and must insist upon staying."

"Oh, Elbert, Elbert, I want to die," she moaned.

"My God, Agnes, is it true that—"

She divined his question, and replied, "No, Elbert, I did not attempt to take the life God gave me; that would be cowardly; but I almost feel like giving up the struggle."

"But, Agnes, you've not told me what the struggle is all about."

"Elbert, it is a secret of the dead," she replied faintly.

"Then I must know. Agnes since you first inspired hope and ambition in me, we've always been honest with each other."

"Yes, until—" she said feebly.

"Now, Agnes, do not drive me away. Tell me as your friend and let me help you," he pleaded.

"Elbert, I am so grieved."

"Agnes, I must know. You owe it to me, and you've done wrong to keep it from me who would have told you all," he said almost sternly.

"Elbert, Elbert, don't wring it from me," she cried piteously.

"Agnes, you're wrecking more lives than one by refusing me your confidence. I'll not betray you."

"Elbert, lean closer—Bart was a murderer. He killed Wesley Walker, and I was his wife," she almost hissed.

"What's that!" he gasped, and he thought it was fever delirium.

"It is true," she continued. "Now leave me to my sorrow."

"Agnes! Agnes!" cried Elbert, bowing his head.

"Bart left a written confession, and I opened it the day you left for Washington," continued Agnes, as if to convince him of the truth.

"Oh, Agnes!" was all that Elbert could say, and their tears mingled in the silence that followed.

"Agnes, let me share your sorrows," continued Elbert, "your life has been so sad."

"But think of it, Elbert. Think of it—Bart a murderer, I a murderer's wife—I almost feel as if I should go mad," said Agnes, excitedly.

"Agnes, you must listen. As your pupil I obeyed you. Now you obey me. Wipe out the past and let me love you."

"Oh, Elbert, I cannot forget."

"Agnes, why divide the ways? Let me love you. My heart is truly yours. Our lives have had their mutual joys and sorrows. Why should we part now?"

She was silent, and Elbert continued:

"But, Agnes, I will not urge farther."

"Mamma Aggie, does 'oo feel better?" and a little curly head peeped in at the door.

The old smile of love was her only response to the child's words.

The invalid improved rapidly, and Elbert felt now that his duty and honor required that he insist upon closer relations, so that he could give Agnes the protection she needed. In sharing her secret the reserve between them had vanished. The presence of Elbert seemed to comfort Agnes, and yet her sensitive nature shrunk from him because of the horrible revelation of Bart's confession. She feared that knowledge of her sorrow had influenced Elbert to reiterate his love, and that he was mistaking sympathy for real affection, and she decided that it was wrong for her to remain there. Ever since the kindergarten had opened and little Veo had been her especial charge, it had been her unconscious ambition to please Elbert. It now came upon her like the breaking of a gentle dawn that she could no longer remain merely Elbert's friend. And his wife?—that could never be.

That night, although scarcely recovered from her illness, she left Poplarville, having determined to find a new home, and break the ties which she feared threatened to mar Elbert's future.

She started out again, alone in the world.

CHAPTER XXXIV.

"**And a little child shall lead them.**"

—Holy Writ.

The disappearance of Agnes was perhaps the greatest sensation known in Poplarville since the day when Daddy Doughtoe blew his head off with a shotgun, with the exception, of course, of the "Snakes" revelation and Abner's sudden disappearance. No one could assign any reason, except Dr. Buzzer, as to why Agnes should have left.

"Overwork and wandered off in a fit of melancholy; always said so."

The sensations seemed to come in groups, and overwork is a convenient explanation of mysterious events, because the affairs of the heart are always disguised from the vulgar gaze of the world.

Elbert was alarmed when he remembered their conversation the day previous, and feared that in a moment of desperation Agnes had taken her life. Every conceivable nook and corner where a suicide would likely have retreated, was searched. The Pinkertons from Chicago looked very wise and said it would take time, and Elbert refused to return to Washington with this state of uncertainty existing. Little Veo could not understand it, and wandered about the house, clinging to her grandma's skirts, piteously crying, "Mamma Aggie, Mamma Aggie." The days passed and no word. Elbert received information of his appointment to a coveted foreign mission, but it did not deter him from his search for Agnes. He had about given up hope of her being alive, and yet something told him that Agnes was too brave to give up life's struggle in that way. Little Veo was taken ill a few days later, and in her raging fever she continued calling for "Mamma Aggie," and every cry seemed to cut the heart of the father like a knife, as he watched by her bedside. Through the long vigils of the night he sat, hoping and hoping that that face would appear to calm the little sufferer. Surely she would not desert him in his hour of sorrow if she only knew. The next day the prosaic want column of a leading Chicago daily was varied by a strange notice. It seemed to tell a life story in itself and the hundreds looking over the page for help stopped and wondered as they read:

TEACHER WANTED—Little V. very low with fever; calls "Mamma Aggie." Come quick or too late. E. will not be there.

Elbert wrote it as a last resort, little hoping for any result. While the fever abated somewhat, the little one kept calling for "Mamma Aggie," until he was almost crazed. A few days later, nearly at dusk, when little Veo was sleeping quietly, Elbert started for a walk. During his absence Agnes came to the house, and she was immediately taken to the sick room by Mrs. Ainsworth. When the little one awoke and recognized "Mamma Aggie," she gave a feeble cry of joy. Agnes sat and stroked her head, and the little one said:

"I knew 'oo would tum, Mamma Aggie, I had such a happy dream.

"Now be quiet, dear," said Agnes softly.

When Elbert returned his mother met him and told him Agnes was there.

"Has she asked for me?" he inquired breathlessly.

"No."

"I promised to stay away and not molest her. Call me, mother, if anything happens."

Like an exile he responded to the call of a neighbor's dinner-bell for that day. He felt content, and yet miserable. Word was brought to him from his mother that Veo was improving, and it was arranged that he should call and see her while Agnes was taking her walk, on the day that he was to return to Washington. He felt like a thief as he approached his home, but when he saw the sweet, thin face of Veo he forgot his hardships.

"My little girl has been so ill; but she's all right now, isn't she?" said the father, patting her hands.

"Yes, papa, what did 'oo bring me?

"Bless your heart; your naughty papa forgot and will go and—"

"No, papa, I'll dess give 'oo sumfin' to-night."

"What is it?"

"Oh, sumfin' 'oo like."

"Can't I guess?"

"No, sumfin' I like, too."

"All right, I'll go to the grocery and see what I can get for the little girl."

"No, papa, you des play with me, hide and seek."

"Is little Veo strong enough?"

"I's all yight, papa," said Veo.

"All right, you hide?"

"No, no; 'oo hide, I'll blind," said the child, clapping her hands in glee.

"But where?" he asked.

"Oh, des anywhere; in the closet, 'hind the door."

"One, two, three, four, five, six, get in quick," said Veo, blinding her eyes on the sofa.

And to humor her he went into the closet. She jumped up and going to the door of the closet turned the key.

"Veo, Veo, let me out," he cried.

"Des a minute, papa, des a minute."

"But I must be ready to leave to-night," he pleaded.

"All yight, papa. Hush, hush," she whispered to him in a mysterious way, as she stood guard over her prisoner.

Just then Agnes came into the room.

"Why, my little girl is looking so well," she said, laying off her cloak and kissing her.

"Mamma Aggie, I love 'oo so!"

"Yes, I know, dear. What were you doing, pet?"

"Des playin'," and she cast a furtive glance at the closet door.

"Mamma Aggie, won't 'oo play b'ind man's buff?" she asked.

"I'm afraid you're too tired, dear."

"No, I isn't," remonstrated the child.

"All right; put on the blind," said Agnes, with mock resignation.

Veo climbed up on a chair and carefully tied the kerchief over her eyes, and then cried in high glee, "Now tatch me, Mamma Aggie, now tatch me."

Agnes with groping hands approached Veo, who stood sentinel by the closet door. She had turned the key, and as her prisoner stepped out, Agnes, in groping for the child, put her hands upon him.

"Elbert," she cried, startled, taking off the kerchief.

"Blind, but now you see, Agnes," he said, taking her in his arms. "Agnes! my own heart, Agnes!" he cried, not waiting a response.